2002

Dear M

Happy

all the love in my heart.

Jane.

XO.

THE LIVES OF
AUSTRALIANS
THROUGH
CORRESPONDENCE

Letters from Our Heart

edited by jennifer campbell

THE AUSTRALIAN

AUSTRALIA POST

Hardie Grant Books

Published in 2002
by Hardie Grant Books
12 Claremont Street
South Yarra, Victoria 3141, Australia
www.hardiegrant.com.au

National Library of Australia
Cataloguing-in-Publication Data:

Letters from our heart.
ISBN 1 74064 053 5.
1. Australians. 2. Australia – Social conditions.
994

Text and cover design by Ruth Grüner
Printed and bound in Australia by McPherson's Printing Group

Every effort has been made to trace copyright holders of the letters. The publishers regret any errors and omissions, and would like to hear from anyone who has any information otherwise.

Contents

INTRODUCTION

In April 2001, *The Australian* published a magazine called *Letters From Our Heart*, part of our contribution to the Centenary of Federation celebrations. The response was overwhelming and unprecedented; this small collection of letters by 'ordinary' Australians had touched readers in a way rarely experienced in newspaper publishing.

When *The Australian* decided to compile a book of the same name, we placed an ad in the paper asking readers to send in their family letters. Again, the response was extraordinary. Thousands of letters tumbled through *The Australian*'s mail room, many of them retrieved from the backs of wardrobes and drawers, or from long-forgotten boxes 'under the house'. They had been handed down from generation to generation, their caretakers dutifully safeguarding them for posterity.

What we had was not an arbitrary collection of private correspondence, but a living, breathing narrative of Australia's social history. This was not the impersonal voice of the history books, but a verbatim account of what life in Australia used to be like.

We had enough letters to fill ten books. After a long and often excruciating process of elimination, we finally settled on 100 for this collection. The letters we have chosen are drawn from every period of our national life: they are written by convicts; soldiers on the killing fields of Europe; husbands and wives; parents. Their words are moving, poignant, often distressing. Through them we discover the culture, ethics and opinions of the day.

We have leaned toward the historical rather than the contemporary in this collection. Did people write better letters pre-phone and fax? Probably. Letters were, after all, their only form of long-distance communication, so great care would have been taken in their construction. Perhaps they simply had more time to spend pondering how to express themselves.

We hope you enjoy *The Australian*'s *Letters From Our Heart* as much as we enjoyed putting it together. During the editorial process, original spellings and grammar have not been corrected, but several letters have been edited due to space considerations. Otherwise, they remain untouched.

Our thanks to the many readers who have shared their treasured family missives with us and allowed us to be relentlessly inquisitive in our quest to put their letters into context. Without their patience, generosity and goodwill, this book would not have been possible.

Letters from Our Heart

ALFRED DEAKIN *was in India when he wrote this passionate letter home to his wife of eight years, Pattie (née Elizabeth Martha Anne Browne). Deakin, who was to become Australia's second prime minister, was travelling on the subcontinent writing articles on irrigation and literature for* The Age *newspaper in Melbourne. He had married Pattie (pictured overleaf) in 1882, when he was 26 and she 19, despite the protestations of her parents, who considered him an impecunious barrister. The couple, who lived in South Yarra, went on to have three daughters, Ivy, Stella and Vera. This letter is held by Mrs Judith Deakin Harley, the daughter of Vera. Alfred, who at the time of writing this letter was interested in spiritualism, died of stroke in 1919 at the age of 66. Pattie, a social reformer who ran the Anzac buffet on St Kilda Road during World War 1, lived until the age of 73, dying in 1934.*

28 December 1890

Dearest of sweethearts & sweetest of wives – no news from you or of you – & I am still dreaming of you day & night. Do you remember the night we were all at the Opera House before we were engaged when I leaned on you & they played 'Soft as the stars that are shining' – Do you remember at Park House when I held your hand in the circles & sometimes passed my palms over your head – Do you remember our evenings alone in the drawing room or that day – that never forgotten day when you came to me on the landing to try on the ring before we went to be married – The evenings in the gardens or on horseback – The happy times in the little front room at Adams St & that other where I found you lying faint & tiny little Ivy in the corner – Mailton when we walked out together – Walsh St when I said goodbye – Llanarth when I rushed upstairs & found you dressing on my return – Our last goodbye at the dining room door; & the other upstairs I remember them all – recall them & dwell upon them – for they are you & alas all I have of you now – I have done with travelling – It costs too much – Too much heart ache – too much anxiety – too much longing – Last night I was whistling & singing 'Waiting' thinking of you singing it at Park House often & especially the night before I went to Fiji – I never thought Park House was so dear to me as I now find it to be – I wonder if any man is as contented with his choice as I am – I have never yet regretted it – never wished it undone – never seen anyone whom I thought

I could have married except you & this after nearly nine years of wedded life with so capricious & captious a being as I am – is it not wonderful! Because it is not as if I am contented that you should be only as you have been as I am always wishing you to grow & be better sweeter & stronger – that is for your own sake & in yourself – for my sake & as regards me I am absolutely satisfied even if you had never developed – I wish you to be a nobler wife & a grander mother & a holier woman but it is not for my comfort & happiness as your husband – I am as happy as I can be loving you & having you while you are happy & well – I am your lover still & as such have no fault to find with you – as your spiritual companion I am critical & often try to open you out – perhaps unwisely – But if you knew how I loved you this would only make you more bright & glad because of the sincerity of the love that is satisfied for itself but never satisfied for you either with itself that is my love or with your soul unless it glows brighter & purer every day – Nothing have I to send or say but love unending & inexhaustible for you & for my darling children – love them for me & from me & tell them how I cherish them & pray for them & you to God morning & night my dearest my angel.

Please keep papers with my articles in – a clean copy of all

Kisses again &
again & always –
Alfred

WILLIAM KERNOT SHENTON *wrote this letter to his cousin Maria in England. It describes the wedding of his cousin George Shenton, 27, to a 17-year-old Anne Cousins in Perth in 1838. George and William had come out from Winchester, England, to seek their fortunes in the Swan River Colony. At the time of his marriage George was making his way as Perth's first chemist. William built and owned the wheat mill at South Perth, which is today a National Trust building and tourist attraction. George and Anne went on to have thirteen children. The letter was contributed by George and Anne's great granddaughter, June Shenton Turner, of Shenton Park, Perth. It is held by the Battye Library in Perth. The portrait of George Shenton overleaf is held by the Royal West Australian Historical Society.*

SYDENHAM COTTAGE
December 5, 1838

Dear Maria,

About two months have elapsed since I last wrote to you a most clear and intelligible account of the loves of your Brother George and the fair damsel Anne Catherine Cousins. I have now the pleasure to inform you that I was present on Thursday last the 29th of November, 1838, at the wedding of the said George and Anne Catherine, the ceremony took place about half past two at George's own house (special licence of course) – present Mr Cousins who gave away his daughter, Mrs Cousins who looked very serious as though she did not like to part with her Annie – Mrs W. Knight who acted as British Woman – W.K.S. as witness to all this wickedness. George went through the awful ceremony very well – the Bride as well as expected – rather too nervous to sign the book on the first attempt but after half an hour's respite succeeded in relinquishing her right to sign that name for ever – indeed she had supposed she had adopted her new one but was instructed by the Parson that her maiden name was the required one – then up steps in all simplicity, Mrs W. Knight who was about to sign her maiden name so we had lots of fun especially in joking the parson who is himself to enter the holy estate some day in the present month – to a Lady some years younger and he is judged to be 50. A regular jolly parson – very dark, reads and preaches well but not at all (nor sufficiently) serious – well it is half past two and the wedding over – a glass of wine, cake, the Register

signed – Parson dismissed for the present with his register under his arm – neighbours staring – window blinds which were down during the ceremony are now drawn up – the bride's cheeks not quite so blushy – in comes a sacey [saucy] boy for some physic – George too busy says, 'Call again tomorrow, I've married a wife and cannot come' – and so somehow dinner time half past five approached – then mustered as follows – Mrs George Shenton at the head of the table supported on the Right by the Parson, Mr Wittenoom, on the left W.K.S. – lower end of table [hole in letter here where the letter was folded – a word or two missing] – George Shenton – Father one side, Mother the other, between on each side married folks and young Virgins – oh how after dinner the almond shells and raisins flew about, we were very merry till near twelve – when in compliments to the Benedicts we drank the 'Pestle and Mortar' and retired, having missed the happy pair some time before.

So there he is now a regular steady old married man – for almost a week has elapsed, but they will not appear at Church till next Sunday. In my last I gave you a full account of the bride – and have nothing farther to add but that she is worthy of all the regard and affection you can bestow as your sister-in-law 'doing as you would wish to be done by' in similar circumstances. I shall have the happy pair to dine with me some day next week, also Mr and Mrs Knight etc. – and I suppose we shall dine together on Christmas day – but at which house I cannot say.

Yours affectionately,
W.K. Shenton

Murderer DENIS PRENDERGAST, *a convict in the harshest of all penal colonies, Port Arthur, wrote this brief letter to his homosexual lover, Jack, just before he was to be executed in 1846, a moving display of tenderness amid wretched suffering. Held by the Archives Office of Tasmania (G033/57). Printed with permission.*

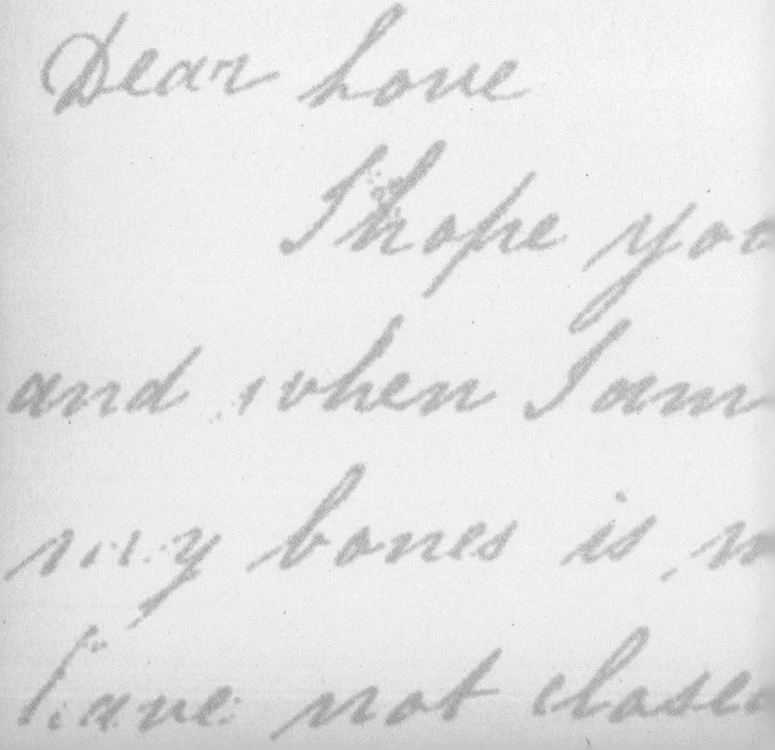
Dear Love
I hope yo
and when I am
my bones is
have not close

1846
PORT ARTHUR, TASMANIA

Dear Love,
I hope you won't forget me when I am far away and all my bones is moldered away I have not closed an eye since I have lost sight of you, your precious sight was always a welcome and loving charming spectacle. Dear Jack I value Death nothing but it is in leaving you my dear behind and no one to look after you. But I hope you will beware of the delusive of man. The only thing that grieves me love is when I think of the pleasant nights we have had together. I hope you won't fall in love with no other man when I am dead I remain your True and loving affectionate Lover.

Denis Prendergast

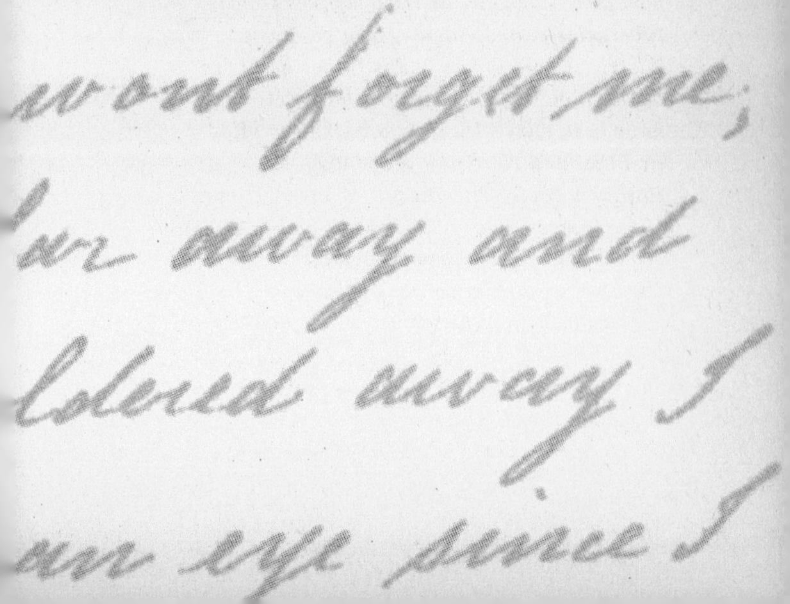

HERBERT CURLEWIS *was a 22-year-old law student when he penned this wounded epistle to Ethel Turner (pictured). Turner, at 21 already a promising young writer, had just spurned his offer of marriage. Despite the letter's air of finality, the couple were engaged two months later. The year was 1891; two years later Turner was to write* Seven Little Australians, *one of Australia's best-loved novels. As Ethel was uncertain of her love for Herbert, and unable to obtain her stepfather's permission to marry, the couple were secretly engaged for five years before going on to enjoy 46 years of marriage. They had two children: Jean, who died tragically at the age of 31 from tuberculosis, and Adrian, who became a District Court judge, as his father had been before him. Many Curlewis family letters have been published in two books compiled by Ethel and Herbert's granddaughter Philippa Poole,* The Diaries of Ethel Turner *(Lansdowne, 1979) and* Of Love and War *(1982). This letter appears for the first time in the 1998 paperback edition of* The Diaries of Ethel Turner.

HERMSLEY
March 5, 1891

Dear Miss Turner,
In answer to your note I have nothing whatever to say except to thank you for the gentleness you showed in doing what you felt to be your duty.

You must not ask me ever to see you again – my pain is now greater than I can bear and I could not trust myself to increase it.

I have various letters and tokens of you that I have not the courage to destroy and so shall ask you to do so for me. I shall ask Creed to give them to you – he knows I never go to your house though he does not know why.

So ends the last letter I shall write to you – God bless you and keep you my darling – you will I know always think kindly of me.

I remain
Yours sincerely
H. R. Curlewis

In keeping with custom at the time, JOHN BLAIKIE *wrote a letter to request the hand in marriage of his sweetheart, Jessie (pictured overleaf), the eldest daughter of John McLennan. The reply, although written in the stilted style of the beginning of last century, exhibits the deep feelings of both parties. The couple had met in 1907 at Swan Hill, Victoria, where John worked for the Commercial Bank. They did not marry until 1913 as officers of the bank were not permitted to wed until they earned a certain salary. When they did marry, John was 29, Jessie 31. They enjoyed 31 years of marriage before John died of a heart attack in 1944 at the age of 54. Jessie lived to the age of 94, dying in 1977. This letter was contributed by Lynette Blaikie, of Brisbane, the wife of Malcolm, one of the couple's four sons.*

PINNAROO, SA
July 17, 1910

Dear Mr McLennan,

You I trust are already aware of the attachment between your dear daughter Jessie and myself. I am writing this letter to ask your consent to our engagement and ultimate marriage.

We have known each other for the past four years and have been keeping company practically ever since, so you will see that my sacred request of you is much more than the outcome of a passing fancy.

While I have not yet had the pleasure of making your personal acquaintance I can count amongst my friends many of your relatives in Louis, Mr Neil McLennan, Mr Louis McLennan of Bulga and Mrs W.G. Wilson.

I have written this latter paragraph as a father would not part with one so dear as Jessie is to you were he not sure of the future happiness of his daughter,

Anxiously awaiting your reply,
I remain
Dear Mr McLennan
(John Blaikie)

Hillhead
BANYENA, VIC
July 25, 1910

Dear Mr Blaikie,

Your letter of the 17th is to hand. I confess that although we have never met I am not taken by surprise at the request you have made. Having heard a great deal about you during the past three years, and what I have heard is very much to your credit.

But in a matter of this kind which involves the future happiness of my dear Jessie I rely more on her good sense and judgment and as it appears that you are mutually attached to each other, my daughter's future happiness being as it were bound up in yours, it gives me the utmost pleasure to consent to your engagement and marriage. At no very distant date I trust to have the pleasure of making your acquaintance.

I am, dear Mr Blaikie,
Yours faithfully,
John McLennan

You can almost feel the ache in JAMES WISEMAN*'s heart as he pens this love letter to his betrothed, barmaid Ada Rymills of the Bridge Hotel, Goulburn, NSW. The couple spent most of their engagement apart as Jim, a shearer, worked the sheds all over NSW.*
While apart they wrote to each other every day, at first love letters full of plans for their wedding, and then letters about their children and the hardships of the Depression. Their letters were recently featured in an exhibition at the State Library of NSW, 'Private Lives: Families of NSW'. This letter and photograph of James and Ada on their wedding day in 1913 are printed with permission of the Mitchell Library, State Library of NSW (ML MSS 6756) and Mrs Vena Croke, a daughter of Ada and Jim who lives in Toukley, NSW.

NEVIE DOWNS
February 22, 1912

My dearest Ada,

Just a line to let you know how I am. Well Ada dear I am far from getting over our parting yet I ought to be ashamed to admit what I am going to tell you the first week that I left I put my hed out the windo of the carriage and loock back at the big train pulling me away from you and the water woad cum out of my eyes like a big babey. O Ada I never thought the parting was to be so hard. Un till I said the lass good bye to you then I knew what it was going to be and my word I have suffered and know yet when ever I loock at my watch I all ways try to emagin what you are doing but it will not be for long Ada I think I will go strat back as soon as I finish here if nothing turns up and wait untill June it is nearly a surt that I will do that as things are in a terrible stait out here. And I am to far away from you. I will go back and wait till june and then go to Mungindi on the border I am nearly 1300 miles from you here and all straing people and there is no one to cheer me or talk to me and then I get by my self and loock at the watch and emagin what you are doing dear Ada. I am a broken hearted man and I hope that you are not the same be case I will be back soon. Well darling Ada I tell you what I met with wen I got to Charleville lass saturday there was not a brest of wind and it was 121 in the shade and they told me that it had not been under 110 for 3 weeks so just emagin how I felt I was farley broken hearted then I had to ride the bike 100 miles in the dust I was not fit to do it so I toock the coach Well then you should have seen the country miles and miles of barren plains no water no grass and stock dieing in thousands this is the only shed in this part of the country.

[Area of text missing as page three of the letter did not survive]

Give my kind regards to your mum and dad

Well Darling good bye Ada O yes I live for you aloan and I will soon be back if things doant aulter or I wood die out here.

Well good bye Ada
Good bye darling
Believe me
yours ever loving
Sweet hart I miss

Rite soon Ada
do not for get
xxxx
your loving
boy Jim

LILA LEHMANN *(née McIlwaine) had just recovered from a near nervous breakdown (known then as 'brain fever') when, still grieving, she wrote about her husband Ben's death three months earlier in World War I, aged 37, to her sister-in-law Helene. A proud Australian, Ben had enlisted in the Citizens Military Forces before the war. He and Lila, pictured here on their wedding day, had been married for nine years, and had no children. Lila remained in Fremantle and never remarried. She died in 1925 at the age of 43. This letter was submitted by Dorothy Gill of Mount Waverley, Victoria, Helene's granddaughter.*

1917
DECEMBER 12
EAST FREMANTLE

Dear Helene,

Please forgive me not answering your kind letter sooner. The loss of my dear husband has been such a dreadful blow that I have not had much thought or inclination for anything. I should I suppose be very thankful that the doctor managed to avert an attack of brain fever, but I am not in a frame of mind to be very thankful for anything. The only thing that seems to matter is that I have lost Ben and I cannot think of anything else. By last mail I had a letter from a friend of dear Ben's telling me that Ben was slightly wounded in the arm and went to the dressing station to have it attended to. The doctor wanted to send him down to the base but Ben's sense of duty was so great that he refused to go and insisted on going back to the line. He was on his way back to rejoin his section when a shell struck him killing him instantly. My poor boy. He was our own dear brave hearted fellow even to the last. Even in my misery Helene, I cannot help saying it was a glorious end to a beautiful life. It is so hard to write of it dear. There are lots of things of interest I could tell you of but I cannot write them. Perhaps some day we will meet and I will be able to tell you. I am still receiving my darling's letters, the last one dated four days before he was killed. I cannot write more, please forgive this scribble. It is so awkward to write sitting propped up on a sofa.

With love
Yours sincerely, Lila

LEILA SELINA CORAL CHANTER *(pictured) wrote this letter to her daughter Leila May (Maise) and husband Harold Fletcher in 1936 after their four-year-old daughter, Nancye, died of meningitis. Nancye, who was ill for just two days before she died, was the youngest of five children. The family lived on a farm in Willowvale, near Skipton in central Victoria. At the time of Nancye's death, grandmother Leila Selina was staying with her only son, Lynn (Albert Lynton), a schoolmaster in Gresford, NSW, and his wife, Belle, and although obviously very distressed, responded immediately. Yet even amid her shock and sadness there's an optimistic little postscript regarding the improving health of her husband. The holder of this letter, Anne McVie of Marcoola on the Sunshine Coast in Queensland, was the sixth child born into the family, four years after Nancye's death.*

C/- PUBLIC SCHOOL RESIDENCE
GRESFORD, NSW
Tues. 28th July. '36

My darlings, Maise, Harold & dear little Sisters and Brother Frank,

My heart goes out to you all in the passing beyond of our darling little Nancye, four years old on the 4th of last May; my youngest Grandchild – my baby grandchild whom I have never even seen and whom I shall never see in this world now; but she is there in the Better Land waiting for me, the first of our families to go; she of course is emphatically better off – no more pain or sickness; oh the dear sweet little soul; because she is one of God's angels now.

But it is you dear Mum and Daddy, Sisters Joan, Nell and Marge and Brother Frank, who shall miss her so intensely – Grandma's heart just aches for you all my dear ones, but God's ways are not our ways so we must pray for guidance, and say 'thy will be done'. Lynn rec'd your wire just as school was coming out this afternoon; and Belle and he came round the side verandah, and told me as gently as he could. It is a shock to us all, my dear ones. Was our Pet ill long? Are there any other cases about?
And how are all of You, I'm anxious to know.

I cannot write much, dears, therefore do please excuse this scribble, with all loving sympathy from

Mother

Isn't it good news that father is getting on so well at last.

KEN MURRAY *wrote this letter to his eldest son, Kevin, aged 9, a few days before he died, at 37, of bowel cancer in 1937. The stoicism and resilience so evident in the letter's tone were typical of Ken's generation. Hardship was to be endured, not resisted.*

Ken was born in 1899 to a farmer in Trafalgar, West Gippsland, Victoria, the only son in a family of six children. He started working for the Bank of Victoria at the age of 14 and apart from two years spent fighting with the AIF in 1917–19, where Ken was injured at Amiens, he continued working with the bank right up to his death, reaching the rank of Assistant Manager of the Dandenong branch.

From 1926, at the age of 27, he was to know fleeting happiness after marrying 25-year-old school teacher Minnie Ethel Keily. The couple had two children, Kevin, to whom the letter is addressed, and John, who was six when Ken died. (The family is pictured overleaf when Kevin was five.) Kevin Murray is now 73 and lives in Balwyn, Victoria. John, who contributed this letter, is now 69 and lives in Ivanhoe. Both are retired teacher's college lecturers.

Dear Kevin,

By the time you get this letter I will be dead and happy amongst the angels, and you will have to take my place as the man of the family.

It seems a big job to put upon the shoulders of a boy as young as you are, but you needn't let it frighten you. You can do your job best of all by being as good and helpful as you can to Mum and by buckling down hard at your school work.

Remember too, that there won't be nearly as much money coming in to the house as there was while I was working, and it will have to be handled very carefully to make ends meet. So take care of your clothes and make them last well, and do not make Mum unhappy by asking for expensive toys which she can't afford to buy you.

I know you will be good to John and see that he is not a worry to Mum.

There is one thing I would very much like you to do for me. That is to try and get over your shyness. I know it's hard, because I was like that myself once. The only way is to make yourself do these things and it's surprising how easy it becomes after a while. If you've got to ask a stranger for anything just go up and do it without thinking over it too much, and speak out clearly, distinctly, because it will only add to your shyness if you have to ask the question again. You will generally find that people are only too pleased to help you.

The time will come in a few years when you will be leaving school and you will have to earn your living. It is not too soon now for you to be trying to get some idea of what kind of work you would like to do. Keep your ears and eyes open and do not be afraid to try your hand at anything you get the chance to do.

Mum has made me very happy by telling me how good you have been since I have been in hospital, and it certainly is a great comfort to me to know that I can die leaving such a good boy to help and look after Mum and John.

Goodbye & God bless you
Your very loving
Dad

BERNARD 'BARNEY' ROBERTS *(pictured overleaf with his first wife Bride and granddaughter Judy) was a gifted man. A keen gardener, fisherman and bowls player and a great raconteur, he was also a skilled teacher. The author of two widely used chemistry and physics school textbooks, he worked for many years at Sydney's Fort Street Boys High School where his pupils included the future governor-general Sir John Kerr. Kathleen, the second of his three children, travelled to Melbourne for a holiday in 1941 and there she met her future husband, Ian Wotherspoon. He, too, was from the Sydney suburb of Epping and both belonged to the Epping Lido Club, a social founded during the Depression. They maintained a long-distance relationship and became engaged on the day Darwin was bombed, 19 February 1942. They married in Epping in June of that year and immediately returned to Melbourne. Judith was the first of their two children, their son John born four years later. After the war, Kathleen and Ian moved from Melbourne to Adelaide, never returning to live in Sydney. Barney died in 1975, aged 86. Kathleen died in May 1998. She was 82. Her daughter, Judith Wotherspoon, is now 57 and lives in Adelaide. The family celebrated its fiftieth year in Adelaide last year.*

1944
TUESDAY, MAY 2
EPPING, SYDNEY

My dearest Kathie,

So now you are the luckiest of women and you have your dear little baby girl with you. It is wonderful. I am thinking at present of you when you were like your dear little Judith Helen, a little baby girl, only a few hours old. Well do I remember the day that happened, and my joy in having you and your dear Mother, both safe and sound, after the trial that every mother must go through to secure such joy that has no equal in the whole of human experience. My present thoughts are of happiness and thankfulness that you are both safe and sound. The words mother and child, both doing well, are sweet music, even to an old grandpa like me.

Sweetheart, I join with you and share in your happiness, as I did on the day you told me you were going to marry Ian. You are, indeed, a fortunate girl – the man you love, the babe you have been waiting for, and your mother with you at the critical time. More than that I am sure you could not desire. So welcome to the new arrival into the family circle, and you have chosen such a pretty name, she will always be dear little Judy to Grandpa Roberts for once more there is a Grandpa Roberts in the family. My darling little girl, I shall be looking forward to seeing you both as soon as possible, but I doubt they would give me a priority at present; you see, being a grandpa is not considered sufficiently important for interstate travel as things are; but perhaps we can find some more satisfactory excuse to the powers that be, later.

By the time you get this I expect and hope you will be well on the way to recovery and what you have been through a memory – perhaps not altogether pleasant, still each time you take dear little Judy in your arms you will say to yourself that it was worth it a hundred times. Your days will be full ones for many years to come.

Now you know what a Mother's love really is and share in what your own mother and father have known so long. Let me recall for you – if you can remember it – one winter's evening nearly 20 years ago in the living room at Mudgee, when you, Dor and I sat in front of the fire, waiting for the news that John was born and Mother was safely through – I am again able to feel the thrill of thankfulness as I then felt it on Mother's account, I now feel it on yours.

Dear old sentimental Daddy, I suppose you are saying to yourself as you read these lines. Well, I am not ashamed of it; for it is a worthy sentiment, at least I think so – for if such times as these did not move us, we should indeed be cold creatures.

So once more my love – the best possible wishes to you my dear one and your darling little daughter. Rest and grow strong again and when you are up once more, keep an eye on your own dear mother, and don't let her overdo it in anyway – for she is, I am sure, just as stirred as I am. Keep her with you until you are well again and able to look after your family and then send her safely home to me – but not sooner. We are quite able to look after ourselves, and there is no need for her to worry about us. Of course when the time comes we shall be looking forward to her return as much as you looked forward to her coming to you. You needed her, and she was able to come, and that is just as it should be, isn't it?

At a time like this I am sure it is the greatest happiness a woman about to be a mother herself can have, that is to have her own mother with her. Give my best love to Ian, and my congratulations on being a father; and a lucky man as well. Kiss dear little Judy for me and don't forget one for yourself. I should just love to be in Melbourne with you myself.

All my best love to you and yours, darling, and all happiness in the future for you three.

Your affectionate Father and Grandpa to Judy

In this letter RAY HAMMOND *pleads with his wife of just one year, Gloria, not to end their marriage. It was Ray's second marriage; his first had broken up while he was serving in the Royal Australian Air Force during World War II. Living with the couple were Ray's two teenage daughters from his first marriage and Gloria's 10-year-old daughter from her first marriage. Gloria did reconsider, and the couple spent the next 47 years together until Ray's death in February 2000 at the age of 87. Gloria, now 81, lives on the Gold Coast, the couple's home since retirement in 1974. Gloria attributes the early hiccup in their married life to the complexities of the 'blended family'.*

November 5, 1952
23 Annandale Street
ANNANDALE, SYDNEY

Dear Gloria,

In the turmoil of leaving last Saturday, there were quite a few things I would liked to have said, but you weren't in a suitable frame of mind to listen, even now I can't really say everything that is in my heart, but it seems a really great shame for our marriage to break up after such a short space of time, just when we were really starting to get to know each other (I thought). Did you really mean it when you used to say that I had to last you for the rest of our lives, couldn't we have a talk and try and iron things out. I am really sincere in writing this Gloria, but if you have really made up your mind you don't want it this way then I am still prepared to stick to my part of our previous arrangement, but please Dear give it serious thought.

I Remain,
Truly Yours,
Ray

MISS ALICE ALLEN *wrote this letter to her niece Barbara Harradine in 1954, just after the birth of Barbara's first child, Geoffrey. Alice had been like a second mother to Barbara and her sister Joyce when they were children. She had moved in with their mother – Alice's sister – Dorothy Evans, after Dorothy was widowed in 1929 while still pregnant with Barbara. Alice ran the home in Surrey Hills, Melbourne, while Dorothy returned to work. Aunt Alice told the two girls that she never married because 'the one she wanted didn't want her and the ones who wanted her, she didn't want'. Alice died in 1969 at the age of 86. This letter was contributed by Barbara Harradine of Somers on the Mornington Peninsula in Victoria.*

5 BORONIA STREET
SURREY HILLS
15.12.54

My Dear Barbara,

I am very pleased that we have a small boy in the family again. It will liven us old girls up again.

You had a pretty long hard row to go, but I guess you think it was worth it all now. You will soon forget the discomfort of it and think only of the joy to come. You and Ian will enjoy your little son.

He will be company for you while Ian is away all day, that will make Ian smile, but mothers and maiden aunts know how much pleasure you can get out of caring for little children. I know for all the pleasure I had in life was what I got out of you and Joyce when you were very young and growing up. I did enjoy you both.

Well, my dear, I hope all your worry and discomfort is over till little sister comes along. You were a real Briton all the way through and we are very proud of you.

Well I must close now.

Lots of love from your old
Aunt

P.S. I found a little pants pattern the other day and I have put it away. With the nice grey material I have been hoarding up for this (it is all new) I hope to be able to make him his first boy pants. I guess you will think I am looking a long way ahead, but they soon grow, in fact they are not born as young as they used to be.

By one who knows.

JOAN PORTER *had been writing a note on her wedding anniversary cards every year since she and her husband 'Chas' (Charles) had moved into their house in the new suburb of Caringbah, in Sydney's south. At that time, they had been married for thirteen years. The Porters (pictured) were a typical postwar family: they had a new house, a new car in the garage, and three happy, healthy children, Suzanne, Michael and the baby, Celestine. The final hurdle to their happiness was cleared when Charles was eventually able to leave the Navy and start working at the Atomic Energy Commission Nuclear Reactor at nearby Lucas Heights, thereby avoiding the lengthy absences that had kept him away from his family. But there was a tragic twist that would destroy their lives together. These letters were contributed by the couple's youngest daughter, Celestine Fenby, of Temagog, on the mid-north coast of NSW.*

Our 12th Anniversary
July 14, 1954

The foundation of our own home is laid and we are standing on the threshold of a new life. For 12 years we've battled in all the usual storms and a few of the unusual too – but we've had a lot of laughter among the tears – and with it all has come a deeper understanding and stronger love for each other than we ever dreamed of twelve years ago. We are facing with confidence the years ahead, and pray that God will grant that they are numerous.

Our 14th Anniverary
July 14, 1956

Well this year we're so broke we can't afford a celebration – but at least we're not miserable. We were going to buy some chooks as a joint present but even that fell through.

However Chas is still as kind and thoughtful to me as ever. He brought this card in with my morning cup of tea.

This year we face separation again. Chas is leaving on the 'Sydney' on the 30th July. It's going to be hard to take after being together for so long. Still we feel now that he can't afford to come out of the Navy even at the end of this term. I wonder what I will write on that subject in '58.

Our children are lovely. Suzanne as big as me and wanting to be an artist. Michael dreamy and grubby but doing well at school and such a lovely boy. Celestine adored by everyone, slightly spoiled, but we just can't help it. She's so pretty and charming. That's all for '56. Sounds dull, but it's good and we're still in love.

Our 15th Anniversary
July 14, 1957

This year we promised ourselves a small celebration, but as usual when the time came, we were too broke. Chas was on leave and we got our garage floor down. Big thrill. Next you know there'll be a car standing on it. Just at present we are sure it will be a '54 Humber Hawk black with red upholstery and Chas will be home with us every day. No more Navy. We even hope now he may get an early discharge and a job he has applied for at the Lucas Heights Nuclear Reactor. Oh how I wish I could see what I will be writing on our card next year! We have had a lot of worry over Suzanne in the past year, but it has all cleared up now and looks as if she'll be OK. She is with the St Joseph Nuns at Arncliffe and doing fairly well. Michael gives us concern with a development of asthma. Celestine is charming us with her chatter. Joan still loves Chas. Chas still loves Joan – and that is the most important thing of all.

Our 16th Anniversary
July 14, 1958

It was a Humber Hawk. Black with green upholstery and even more glamorous than we ever dreamt of this time last year. Chas did get the job. He is reactor foreman at Lucas Heights, and I am out there too pounding away at a comptometer. It brings in a few extra pounds but I am not so very pleased with the job and hope to have another one at Parke Davis this time next year.

The past year has been most eventful. What a performance I had to put on to get Chas out of the Navy – but wasn't it worth it. I still can't quite believe I shall see him every day for the rest of our life – but I think it's wonderful and I hope he feels the same way. Our life and our love grow, so deep and beautiful the only thing that mars it is my silly fear that it might be snatched away from me and so break my heart.

Our family is growing up fast. Suzanne is still at Arncliffe but breaking her neck to leave school. She is a typical difficult to handle teenager. But she'll grow out of it. Michael is still a grub but very lovable and devoted to his baby sister. Celestine goes to daily nursery school at Mrs Cheeseman. Adorable, sweet, good and exasperating all at the one time.

We love each other and each other's company. We work and have fun together and that's the way we want to keep it. To this end we are now looking to join a club so we can make more friends.

Life is good and while I wouldn't like to relive the strife of the past sixteen, I'd still do it to have Chas at my side to enjoy the next and the next and the next.

[Added later]

10/7/59

The End.

6 MERCER RD
ARMADALE, VIC
July 23 1959

My darling Joan

How are you? Joan what a tragedy our dear Chas to be taken when he was so happy. I just can't believe it. God's ways are not our ways & at least he did not suffer. [He died of a heart attack.] After all we all have to face death. He is alright but you dear who is left must bear up & put your trust in God & thank God you have a very keen interest in your three lovely children. I will always see Chas coming in the Navy uniform with a bottle for me. We all loved him Joan but I doubt if ever a man loved his wife or home as he did. May God have mercy on his soul may he rest in peace. It gives me great comfort to know you & the children are so religious & good. Irene is still very weak & sick she does not relize how bad she is or that there is no hope of her getting better. She has never been told. Don't ever mention it is hopeless in her's or my letters, we always read each others' letters. The shock of Chas upset us very much all that night but we calmed down a good bit next day. Allie was over yesterday to tell us all about the funeral, what a terrible day it was. Pleased to hear Celestine is taking it so well, I was a bit afraid of her she loved her daddy so much & oh how he loved her.

Now I know you will be brave as you know what is ahead of you. God is good so put your trust in him & you have very good children.

God bless you all I will be praying for you all the time. Irene finds it almost impossible to concentrate on writing but is thinking of you all the time.

Love from us both

Your loving Mother xxxxx

CORRY DE HAAS *of Helensvale, Queensland, received this letter in 1960 shortly after moving to Australia from the Netherlands with five small children. At the time she was living in an immigration hostel in Brisbane. After a newspaper ran a story on the family (pictured), Mrs Alison Luxford, a complete stranger, wrote to wish them a good life in their new country. 'It gave me really good hope for the future,' Corry de Haas, who contributed this letter, says today. 'It has been a wonderful time. The first few years were difficult and I was very busy with a big family but on the whole when I look back on it, Australia is home. When we drive through the country, that's when I write poetry. When I see films on the outback I am moved to tears. It feels as if I should be here.'*

1960
MAY 26
Sth Murwillumbah, NSW

Dear Mrs de Haas,

I love your photo and those lovely children and I think Monica, the one closest to you, is you over again. I keep saying to my family, 'Oh, isn't this a lovely mother and family.'

I hope and pray that God will bless you and your husband and those little children in this, your new country, are the sincere wishes of an old grandma.

All the best,
(Mrs) Alison A. Luxford

Geoffrey Morris was just four years old when he received these two letters from his mother, MARY JEAN MORRIS, *who was in St George Hospital in Kogarah, Sydney, dying of breast cancer. Geoffrey, who is now 45 and a scuba-diving instructor living with his wife and three children at Airlie Beach in Far North Queensland, was the youngest of three children and was staying with his grandparents in Belmore, Sydney. He had forgotten all about the letters until he came across them among his father's papers after his father, John Keith Morris, died two years ago. One of his few memories of his mother was of sitting on her lap listening on the radio to Hi Jinx win the Melbourne Cup in 1960. She died the following year.*

1961
ST GEORGE HOSPITAL, SYDNEY

My Darling Geoffrey
I hope you are being a good boy and doing all that you are told.
Dad tells me that you won't eat much for your dinner and tea. If you want mummy home from hospital quick you had better eat a big dinner and tea so I won't be worried.
I went for a big ambulance ride again today.
I went over the big Sydney harbour bridge.
Don't let the dog in the house will you Geoff. That's a good boy.
Have you been swimming in your swimming pool lately.
Did dad give you the little car that the nurse sent home for you.
Mum is very tired now and is going to have a sleep.

Love and kisses and a great big hug
from your loving mummy

p.s give grandma and granddad a big kiss for me

From your loving Mummy
xxxx

1961
ST GEORGE HOSPITAL, SYDNEY

My darling Geoffrey

Well here's another letter from mum at last.

Do hope you are being a good boy and eating all your dinner up.

The better you eat all your dinner the sooner I'll be able to come home. Hope the dog isn't getting in the door and going in side. I'm leaving you to look after him for me.

Be a good boy for grandma and granddad and do as they tell you.

I've got some lollies a lady gave to me for you, so I'll give them to dad to take home.

Wasn't dad dressed up like a sore toe today love. He looked good didn't he.

I must go to sleep now and so had you.

Love and kisses to my little boy
From his loving mummy

JOANNE TUCKERMAN *(known to her family as Joan) never knew her father, Jack, pictured below on his wedding day with her mother, Velia. She was four years old when she and Velia received notification of his death, at the hands of the Japanese, in June 1945.*

When Joanne turned 21 in 1961 her uncle, Kenneth Tuckerman, Jack's elder brother, took the opportunity to tell her what a marvellous, happy, energetic and popular young man her father had been. Joanne took this letter to a family reunion in 2000; until then, Kenneth's own children never knew of its existence. It was contributed by Kenneth's daughter, Barbara Tuckerman of Toowong, Brisbane. Kenneth died in 1973, aged 65. Joanne has this letter framed in her home in Petrie, Queensland. Velia remarried in 1950 and had another daughter, Vicki Archer. Velia died in 1988.

1961
DECEMBER 11
BURWOOD, NSW

Dear Joan,

Enclosed please find your somewhat belated 21st Birthday present and with it goes my best wishes for your future happiness. I would like you to think of it not only as a present from me, but also from your Father whom I am sure would have been very proud of his daughter, if he had lived to see you reach your majority.

We were very proud of your Dad. He belonged to that generation who when they left school had few jobs to go to, and those that obtained jobs, had to work very hard for low wages. When they were about 21, war broke out, and many of them spent the best years of their lives rotting in some prison camp or jungle.

All of Jack's close personal friends died in the war and it is fitting that we should remember them with pride and gratitude for it was by sacrificing these young men, we gained the time to prepare, and eventually defeat our treacherous and cruel foe.

Jack was 14 years younger than me, and we were always great mates. I taught him to swim and surf, and I never knew him to be bad tempered or unkind to any person. He had a perpetual grin that never came off.

He seemed to sense that his life would be short, and he packed as much sport and enjoyment into each 24 hours as possible – taking any hard knocks with unshakable good nature.

I remember on one occasion at a surf carnival Jack competed in every event. First a surf race, then a beach sprint, next the pillow fight and so on. His infectious smile caught the fancy of the spectators and they all started to barrack for him. In the last event he finished dead last, absolutely exhausted, and only just able to crawl up the beach, but everybody cheered him.

During the Depression I saw him do anonymously many kindly actions for his unemployed mates. On one occasion, an unemployed man's kiddy was playing with a rocking chair-horse. I admired the toy, and the child's father told me Jack had bought it. It cost him a week's pay. Yes, he was quite a guy your Dad. When war broke out Jack volunteered. His no. was 34112 and being a typewriter mechanic, I suggested to him that he could obtain a safe job in the army in his technical capacity. He told me that the army wanted to transfer him but he preferred to serve in a fighting unit and not leave his mates . . . the 2/15th Regiment attached to the ill-fated 8th Division.

This unit achieved one of the few successes of the Malayan campaign and cut to pieces the crack Japanese Imperial guards at the Muar River. For this when captured at Singapore many of the 2/15th were tortured and massacred.

I met a man who was in Changi prison camp with Jack and he told me that Jack's constant cheerfulness and unselfishness was an inspiration to all. He was one of the best-loved men in that terrible prison. Finally Jack with 1500 other Australians was transferred to Sandakan Borneo. With the war almost over the Japanese drove these 1500 living skeletons on the infamous Sandakan death march. Only five survived.

Jack died when he was about 24 years, and although he was starved, tortured, and finally driven to his death somewhere in the jungles of Borneo, I'll bet they never broke his spirit.

Perhaps this will make you sad, I hope proud of your Father, and as an excuse for this long letter I think that these men, their exploits, and what they suffered should be made known to their children, who through their sacrifices are now living in such good times and enjoying this wonderful land of ours as free men and women, instead of being under the heel of a foreign conqueror.

Once again I extend to you my very best wishes on attaining your majority, and wish you all the very best for the years that lie ahead.

Your loving Uncle Ken T

HELENE CHUNG *was the ABC's first female foreign correspondent when she was posted to Beijing (then Peking) in June 1983, aged 38. The dream job, however, put immense strain on her relationship with John Martin, her partner of seven years. He took a year's leave from his job at the Victorian Education Department to join her in Beijing in 1984, and they subsequently spent three weeks together in Australia in August 1985. This letter, written two months later, follows a Melbourne–Beijing phone call in which John had said their relationship was damaged. The couple (pictured overleaf) remained together, however, and Helene returned to Melbourne in 1986.*
They married in 1992. A year later, John died of cancer. Helene remains in Melbourne. She is the author of Shouting From China *and* Gentle John My Love My Loss, *and is working on a volume of correspondence, 'Tasmanian Tigers Distant Dragons – Love and Letters From China', which intertwines politics and travel with a love story.*

1985
SUNDAY OCTOBER 6
PEKING P.R.C.

Darling John,

I am truly troubled by what you have told me, but after hearing what I did, agree that you are taking the right action. From so far away, I feel so helpless. I am sorry too that my job seems to have caused the problem. I know that I do tend to assume/hope there must be solutions to problems whereas in fact some problems have no answers. But I do hope that even by now you are feeling a little better, and on the way to becoming yourself again.

Whatever you do, you have my full support. My only concern is that you feel well again – whether with or without me.

I thought that my returning to Peking, deciding to stay on here, was a joint decision. Be that as it may, I don't suppose that either of us realised what we were doing to our relationship. I remember shortly after I first arrived, and I told someone that you were coming later to join me, the person said: that's good, long distance relationships don't last.

As you know you are always in my thoughts. You were the one man I loved for almost 10 years, the first man I was to fall 'in love' with. And I still remember that surge of excitement, that feeling of completeness in simply being with you, the snatched caresses and kisses in the kitchen in Geelong in between preparing dinners for guests by the fire. In the intervening years, we have built up a life together I don't think should be lightly put aside.

That makes me well with a sense of loss and sadness.
But we no longer seem to share that magic spark to ignite each other. At times recently too we seem to have been more irritated than comfortable let alone delirious in each other's company. I don't know what this means. It may mean that it is time for us each to go our separate ways, or it may mean that we are going through a problem patch that we will overcome. It would be strange indeed after so long not to experience at least one such problem.

But I don't want us to be bound together by duty

or responsibility. If we are to be together it must be because we both want to be.

This is not a farewell, but a letter to assure you that I understand whatever you may do. I am, too, confused by what has happened.

When you first went back to Australia from Peking, I was absolutely devastated. My life and work here seemed to have no purpose. I cried for weeks. I wondered what I had condemned myself to. Without you, everything was meaningless.

But gradually I realised that it was not the end, that we would be seeing each other regularly, and that after the posting, we would be together again. Indeed during the posting, I had hoped that you would be able to return. And with the pressure of work, I was forced to put myself back into the job – even without you here – and my day to day life became more tolerable, and often professionally rewarding though personally incomplete. And because of the professional camaraderie, together with the full work program, I was more able to cope than you with the separation.

Our years together were the best in my life, the time when I most felt like a person. To me, it was wholly satisfying. Whether we are to share a life together in the future, or whether that is not to be, you know that I will always love and care for you.

Wo Wo.

19:30 – Over the past 24 hours since we first talked, my overwhelming feeling has been one of utter loss and emptiness at the mere thought of a permanent separation. I need you back here as soon as possible. I think we should be together.

Here is the last letter in a series of correspondence between KEITH RICHARDS *(pictured overleaf) and his beloved aunt Maude. It began after Keith, who had not seen his aunt for forty years, tracked her down to a nursing home in Melbourne. He was 60 and writing a thesis for his arts degree. She was 95 and, although still sprightly, had been in the home for twelve years. Their correspondence continued until her death eighteen months later in 1992. Although they had lived vastly different lives and disagreed on some subjects, they had a close relationship that was of deep importance to both of them. Keith, now 70, has retired to Ropeley, Queensland.*

1992
MAY 23
GLENUNGA, SOUTH AUSTRALIA

Dear Auntie Maude,

This letter is really not for you at all and you will probably never read it. I am writing it for myself because I am having difficulties coming to terms with the fact that a very dear friend is slipping away from me and I have lost contact.

I hadn't realised how much I looked forward to your letters and the way you chastised me for not writing to you often enough. I gave up trying to explain that my work and my study often left me with little time to write. And when I did write, often out of guilt, it would be well after midnight. Those problems seem trivial now because I know that no more letters from you will come to my letter box.

Over the last weeks there have been so many things that I have wanted to share with you, and I have often caught myself thinking that I must tell Auntie Maude – but then I realised with sadness that you could no longer read my letters, and no longer respond to my exploits and my rebellious thoughts.

I would have loved to have told you how today I went ballooning; told how we took off at dawn in fog and then rose majestically through the misty blanket until we broke through into clear sky and saw the sun just being born to another day. Cut off from the world and just floating quietly and peacefully in a boundless space. I thought of you and wondered if this was the same space that you were slipping into and whether your soul was quiet and at peace.

We've talked so often in our correspondence on what was out there beyond death. You were the believer, and me the sceptic. Now you are encompassing your beliefs while I am still left to wonder. You made me face up to many things and the frankness of your questions left no room for complacency. I just had to tackle the issues you put to me. Why has our relationship been so short? Why did I not come to you earlier? Why did I come when I did? I cannot grieve, but only be thankful. Our brief time was so fulfilling. I miss you, my dear friend. I miss the challenge and I miss the expectation of being allowed to take you out next Christmas. It was a hard-won promise.

Vale, Auntie Maude. Your indomitable spirit will stay with me for a long time to come, and I am sure with many others.

My love extends to you wherever you are – now and forever,

Keith

150 Years
of unbroken Service
to
AUSTRALIA
PMG

WIN ELLIS *wrote this letter to Joyce Warry after hearing the news that Joyce's mother, Hylda Warry (pictured as a young woman), had died. Win and Hylda had been lifelong friends, growing up together in Wangaratta, Victoria, and working in the district's wool mills as young women. Despite marrying and going their separate ways, the pair never lost touch, and corresponded every week for more than 70 years. Hylda, who was six months older than Win, died in August 1999. Win died three months later, just before Christmas 1999. This letter was contributed by Joyce Warry of Apollo Bay, Victoria.*

ST CATHERINES HOSTEL
FORD STREET, WANGARATTA 3677
Sunday 12th, 1999

Dear Joyce,

Many, many thanks for your letter telling me of Mum's death.

Has broken a big link for me. Have been writing since 1929, seems a life time, with many happy memories over all our young days.

So one by one old friends are parted and I'm sure you'll miss her.

I'm happy here but no place like home to move around in and do what you want to.

I'll often think of you and thanks again for your kindness.

Kind regards,
From an oldie
Win Ellis
Just had my 95th. Hoping to see 2000 come in.

Letters from Our Past

SIR ROBERT MENZIES *(pictured overleaf) wrote this letter to the captain of the Australian cricket team on the eve of the 1964 Australian Test tour to England. Captain Robert (Bobby) Simpson had asked the Prime Minister for some tips on public speaking. Menzies, a gifted orator and well-known cricket enthusiast, obliged with this carefully written missive. Despite being a staunch monarchist, he urges Simpson not to be apologetic for being Australian. Australia went on to win the series 1–nil. This letter is held in the National Library of Australia (MS 4936/22/13). Printed by permission of the Council of the National Library of Australia and Mrs Heather Henderson of Yarralumla, ACT.*

25 MARCH 1964.

MY DEAR BOB,

I enclose a few copies of things that I have spoken and written which may help you in your tasks as Captain of Australia.

But I really think the best thing I can do for you is to set down in this letter a little broad advice, based upon much experience.

On the occasions when you will be called upon to make a speech in England, your audience will represent a pretty fair sample of English cricket-players and cricket-lovers, with, every now and then, somebody quite famous from Prince Philip and the Prime Minister down.

Don't make the mistake of striving for effect. Just be yourself; speak your own mind and use your own natural language. I learned long ago that the English are more disposed to judge a man on his own merits, and accept him if he rings true, than almost any other race on earth. You will not encounter snobbery among intelligent people. Nor will they seek to patronise you. The only social embarrassment you are likely to encounter will arise from that fact that, as you are a Captain of Australia, you will find yourself prominent on some occasions when your own modest instincts would make you wish to be obscure.

There are some silly and snobbish Australians (very few, I am glad to say) who think that the right way to recommend themselves to their English hosts is to conceal or apologise for their own country. They defeat their own ends. In England there is

a growing interest in Australia as a country quite different from England. Don't hesitate to tell them about your own country and background. Tell them about our Grade and Sheffield Shield competitions, so different from the incessant County cricket over there. Tell them of the excitement that a young batsman experiences when, playing for the first time in the first eleven of his Club, he finds himself facing the bowling of a famous Australia Eleven Star! Explain how this develops our promising players early and quickly.

As you know, I believe that there is something historically special about playing for Australia against England. It was your own ambition, and is that of many others. For England was the cradle of cricket. It gave cricket to the world, and to Australia in particular. Say this. It is true, and it will be warmly received.

In England they are a little worried about the decline in the attendances of County Matches, and are tempted to feel that only repeated visits from the West Indies can save the game. Nothing could have a better effect on their spirits than for you to express your own belief that the game will go on, and that your own team will help in its growth. Speak about your young and comparatively untried players, and say that you believe that they will make a great contribution to the immortality of the game.

Have something to say about the beauty of England, of the thrill of playing at Lords or the Oval, or Trent Bridge; of meeting the great players of yesterday, of being in the land of our ancestors, from which the good and great things in Australia are derived.

[R.G.Menzies]

DAVID SMITH *of Laggan Dam, Scotland, the son of a shepherd, arrived in Melbourne on the* Tasmania *in October 1853, aged 21. His letter marvels at how easy it is for a hardworking man to get ahead, and how quickly Australians are to stand up against an employer who oversteps his authority. These two great tenets of Australian culture – equality of opportunity and a larrikin disrespect for authority – were already well established in the young colonies.*

David (pictured) had eleven brothers and sisters back in Scotland, and by late 1857 the whole clan and their parents had migrated. David bought a farm, which is now the Yarra Valley Park at Templestowe just outside Melbourne, and his brothers George and James built stately homes, Ben Nevis and Sunnyside respectively, both of which survive and are significant houses in the district. Former National Party leader Ian Sinclair is a great-grandson of another brother, Thomas Smith.

This letter is held by Graeme Murphy of Korora, NSW, a great-grandson of another brother, Sam Smith.

1853
NOVEMBER
TO BE CALLED FOR, VICTORIA

My dear parents

I arrived here safe and in good health after a voyage of 88 Days Sailing. We hoisted anchor 27th of July and cast anchor on 23rd of October and lay in the cast anchor about 7 miles from Melbourne owing to the river yarra yarra being so shallow and narrow. But in a few years time the largest ship will get into the new interior warfage place. They intend making a new one in the point of the Bay and a railway to rune from Melbourne to this point.

That Day that we landed there was between 3 and 4 hundred landed on Melbourne Warfe so you would think that everyone could not get employment at once. But any man woman or childe head not been 2 days inclined to work. This is not the Country fore lazy people or Gentlemen but an industrious sober man can do well hear at least 3 times better than at home. Wages is good and employment plenty and clothes cheap almost as cheap as at home. But provisions very high if you go to a Board and Lodging house you will pay from 25 to 35s per week and uncomfortable at that rate.

There is little or no comfort hear. They live more like a set of Tinkers never above a week at one place at least a great many of them. If their master or overseer says a single word amiss they demand their wages and starts off with his Beed clothes on his shoulder, and, before five hours elapses when Masters wanting men soon spy the swag as they call them bed clothes in a bundle and comes up and says, well young lad do you want a job? Yes says he what wages do you give. 30 bob a week. I'll give you more if you will engage for 6 months or 3 months, this is the time that farmers want to engage people now for 3 months or 6 months because they want to have them for their harvest and summer work, for men runs a trip up to the diggings when the wether is fine and dry.

We have very changeable wether hear in the morning some time you would think that it would be a very wet day and in half an hour the sun would be shining and a Beautiful Day, and on the other hand the finest day might in 20 minutes rain the heavist rain that ever I saw. It is also hot during the day and coole all night and a very heavy Due falls by night.

There is nothing pays as well hear as a garden near the town you can get as much manure as you like for nothing even payed for taking it away out of their way, but will in a few years be the reverse fore their will soon be a good deal more land cultivated. The price of vegitables hear as I should know write well the prices of them as that is my Chief employment taking them 2 a week to the market in Melbourne onions 3s 6d per dozen, small ones about the size of a marble 3s per doz. Cabich about the size of your fist 8d each Cauliflowers very inferior 1/- each, flowers per Bunch as many as would gow into the neck of a common bottle is a rose white or red in the Bunch 1/- a bunch the fruit such as oranges the best 6d. each and everything in proportion milk what I have seen give in a small bowl for 1/2d. It Brings 2s hear Butter from 3/- to 2/6 per lb Beef 5d to 6d. Mutton from 41/2 to 51/2d per lb.

And Ile give you a scetch of my voyage. The first 3 days most of us sea Sick owing to us being lands men and not being accostomed to the sea but we all soon got regular golly tars and the ruffest sea after than would not have the least effect upon us, but fortunately I may say we never had a wild day and another Great comfort trouble never approached our Dwelling which is a great Blissing either on land or on Sea. 7 infants Died on the voyage with misels the oldest 6 years of age there were 3 Births.

It is wonderfull how people passes the time there is always something new every day occurring on Board a ship and when fine Clear moon light nights there we had our fiddler up on Deck and he kept musick to thee Dancers. The Irish men had their fiddler and the German jews had their fiddler and Ill leave you to consider what a throng it was on dec and noise fit to deave a person. We had a good supply of Bisqts of the Best Ship or Sea bisqts. We had more of everything than we could use.

I remain your affectionate son.
D. Smith

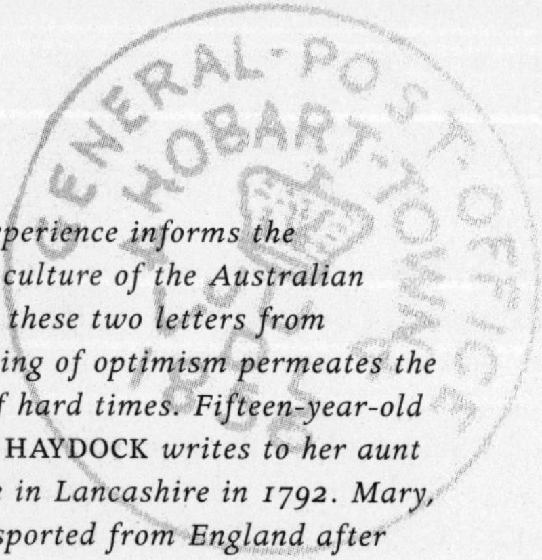

The convict experience informs the character and culture of the Australian nation. But in these two letters from convicts a feeling of optimism permeates the descriptions of hard times. Fifteen-year-old convict MARY HAYDOCK *writes to her aunt Penelope Hope in Lancashire in 1792. Mary, who was transported from England after being convicted of horse-stealing at the age of thirteen, went on to marry Irishman Thomas Reibey. When he died in 1811 Mary, who is featured on the Australian twenty-dollar note (pictured), inherited his thriving grain transport company and went on to become a successful businesswoman in her own right, as well as a vocal emancipist. Letter reprinted with the permission of the Mitchell Library, State Library of NSW (ML MSS5934). Printed by permission of the Library Council of NSW.*

Then there is THOMAS HABERD, *a recently freed convict, who writes to his brother in England in 1846. Thomas wants his brother to know he regrets his behaviour in England and longs to be told if his mother is still alive. Letter reprinted with permission of the Archives Office of Tasmania (NS1275).*

Sydney Town
October 8, 1792

My Dear Aunt,
We arrived here on the 7th and I hope it will answer better than we expected for I write this on Board of ship but it looks a pleasant place – Enough we shall but have 4 pair of trowser to make a week and we shall have one pound of rice a week and 4 pound of pork besides Greens and other Vegetarbles the tell me I am for life wich The Governor told me I was but for 7 years wich Grives me very much to think of it but I will watch every oppertunity to Get away in too or 3 years. But I will make myself as happy as I Can In My Pressent and unhappy situation. I will Give you Futher satisfaction when I Get there and is setted. I am well and hearty as ever I was in my life I Desire you will answer me by some ship that is Coming and lett me know how the Children is and all inquireing frinds. So I must Conclude because we are in a hurry to go a shore remember My Love to my sister and aunt Wamsley and My Cousens. So no more at pressent from your Dutifull neice Mary Haydock. Mr Scot Took 2 Ginnues of me and said he would Get me My Libberty with my sister has been very ungrat To me so I must never see you again.

1846
MARCH 15
HOBART TOWN
TO EDMUND HABERD, FLEET STREET, WINDSOR, BERKSHIRE, ENGLAND

Dear Brother,

I have again taken the favourable opportunity of writing to you hoping it will find you in the enjoyment of good health and doing well as it leaves me at present. It is now about 3 years since I wrote to you before but not having received an answer I expect the letter has been mislaid and lost. You must not think me unmindful of you all for not sending before for almost as soon as I came in this country I got a very bad Master who very soon had me sent to a penal settlement called Port Arthur there I received some very severe hardships, which by the assistance of the Almighty I endured for seven years never forgetting to pray to him who knoweth the very secrets of our hearts for my poor dear Mother and Brothers and Sisters all, whom I hope are alive and doing well.

Dear Brother I am doing pretty well. I am married and got a good wife and one child born last Christmas day a little boy my wife is a native of Suffolk. I am now living on a farm with a young man named Norman Crocker he is a single man and we are quite comfortable though this country is in a very bad state at present. I have got my freedom but not to leave the country. My two companions Henry Bale and James Swain are doing pretty well in Hobart Town if you see any of John Bennets friends tell them he has paid the last debt of nature and it is to be hoped better off in heaven as he was verry steady when alive. I did hear dear Brother our dear

Mother was no more if so I hope her poor dear soul is at rest with our fathers in Heaven, send me word as soon as possible how your are all getting on. I suppose you are all married except Charles. O that I could once more see all then should I think myself the happiest of men send me word how Mr Robert Sebbots family is and tell him when you see that I have often thought of his goodness to us all and what a mad fool I must have been not to behave myself in a proper manner towards him. Tell him also if I forgot his kindness then I do not now but Heartily pray to the Almighty to bless and prosper him, Dear Brother things in this country are about the same as in England. Give my kind love to my dear Mother if she is alive and Mary, Ann, George, Sarah and Charles tell them all I shall never forget to pray for them. My wife also sends her love to you all you must forgive me for not writing before. Give my love to Aunt Hannah and Uncle John and all other relations and friends. I must conclude with my love to all

Your kind and long lost Brother,
Thomas Harberd

When you write to me direct for me at Norman Crockers, Hobart Town, Van Diemans Land.

JOSEPH BLUMSON *(pictured) wrote this letter to his mother in 1898, his first letter home after striking out on his own at the age of sixteen. Joe, the second of twelve children, had left his Adelaide home bound by ship for Fremantle and the Kalgoorlie goldfields in Western Australia. It was the height of the Depression and jobs were scarce. Joe didn't strike it lucky and at eighteen he sailed to South Africa and joined a British regiment to fight in the Boer War. Joe's letters home over thirteen years have been collected into the volume* Voice From the Past: The Life and Letters of Joseph William Blumson 1881 to 1937, *edited by Garry Mighall and published by the Centre for Professional and Public Communication, University of South Australia 2001. This letter is printed with the permission of Beryl Skinner, of Gawler East, South Australia.*

SUBIACO
13 February 1898

Dear Mother and etc,

I have arrived all right after a very pleasant voyage. I enjoyed the trip very much, and I was not sick though nearly all the others were. I turned up at every meal though the food was very rough and the meat tainted and the bread sour. The bad food was thrown out of the portholes sometimes plate and all by the men. There was a concert on board every night in which some good talent was shown. Some of us went up in saloon quarters on Monday night for to liven the saloon up a bit, they need it too – there was better talent by far in the sewerage – that's what we call it – than in the saloon. We got in the piano room and had a few songs till the skipper said we were not to go in that part of the saloon. We went down to the steerage again where it was much livelier. I have seen M Davies a few times and he has given me his address at his sister's, Mrs G Herd. He was very sick on Sunday. There was some Chinese children on board and they were ill. Report got about that it was smallpox, leprosy or measles but the latest I heard it was want of soap and water. They had not had a wash since they left Melbourne. The men are very good at the table and they pass everything you want if you ask for it. We arrived at Albany 10 pm on Wednesday and though it was late we all went ashore and had a look around. I liked the look of the town very much, the hills around on all sides made it look very nice. We left at about 3 o'clock. We did not call at

Bunbury. The Captain said that he did not have orders to call there. They will pay the expenses of the Bunbury passengers and tranship the cargo. The coast between Albany and Freemantle is very pretty, we had it rough for a while near Cape Leuwin. I saw a school of porpoises and some flying fish. We landed at Freemantle 12 o'clock on Friday. Jack was not there to meet me, he was too late so I went on to Subiaco. I enquired for Crompton's and I met one of his men who directed me. I carried my portmanteau for two miles through the bush and sand along a track made by drays. When I got there no one was at home. I waited a quarter of an hour and then Mrs Crompton came in and I was made welcome.

I could hardly speak I was so thirsty. The water here is better than the Adelaide water. The Crompton's are very nice and so is Jack. I slept in a tent with Jack. They have nine horses and four drays and employ two men. Saturday morning I went to Perth to take those things to Miss Macher. She got me lemon squash and wanted me to eat something but I had just had breakfast so I refused. I then went to Freemantle and found Miss Page. I found out her business place – she would not have been home. Her place is very small.

Freemantle is busier than Adelaide. There is about a hundred men to one woman there while at Perth twenty men to one woman. Half the people seem to live in tents. The view from the railway carriage is like your hills only there is more sand and tents of all kinds, bag houses being the common place. The railways over here are better than Adelaide as far as management is concerned. They are narrow gauge. After I left Miss Page I fossicked out the Barker's. It was a good way and they were almost unknown. I asked about twenty people within half a mile and they had never heard the name. I asked the butcher three doors off and he did not know them. I then asked a bootmaker and he said he thought it was next door. He was right and I had found them at last. They were all well and I stayed to dinner and tea. I then found my way back to North Freemantle and Subiaco.

Mr Barker is going to ask for a job tomorrow at the Loco. He says I would get 5/- or 6/- a day – he is getting 13/1 and his brother 12/- per day. They pay 16/- a week rent for three rooms and a kitchen. Mrs Barker says you must excuse her for not writing. She has not had time. She got a paper ready to send but it was put away and forgotten. I am going down to Mr Barker Monday to see whether I'm to work for the Gov – if not I will go and look up Northam. There is no work in Perth.

There are more ads for work than for workers, it seems to be all girls wanted, in one paper there was even about 100. They advertise for boys at about 15/- or 20/- at the Registry Offices but they want a deposit and there are so many frauds that I leave them alone.

My money will soon go if I stay in town and it will last longer in the country. There are plenty of fleas, mosquitoes and flies here and I have got a lot of bites. I am writing to Mr Andrews now and I will write to Will tomorrow and let him know about the Government job. He will let you know. Excuse lead pencil – no time for ink. I am sending prices of things in Perth. Love to all.

I remain your affectionate son
Joe.

In this letter, the visit of the Duke (later George V) and Duchess of York to Australia to open the first federal parliament of the young nation in Melbourne in May 1901 is described in great detail. It was written by 25-year-old ETHEL SHAW, *of Albert Park, Melbourne, to Gertie Hindmarsh, who lived on Rawbelle, a cattle property near Monto, Queensland. Gertie had recently become engaged to Ethel's brother Jack.*

Ethel (pictured in the rear row on left) describes the dresses for an official function as being black. The court was still in mourning for Queen Victoria, who had died at the age of 81 in January 1901, just three weeks after Australia was proclaimed, under her signature, to be a nation. Ethel went on to marry the Reverend George Mackie Baird in 1904 and had three children. She remained in Melbourne for the rest of her life, dying at the age of 74 in 1948. This letter was contributed by Alison Campbell of Bardon, Brisbane, a granddaughter of Gertie and Jack Shaw; the original is held by Amy Shaw, a daughter of Jack and Gertie.

'COOMINGLAH'
ALBERT PARK
SOUTH MELBOURNE
June 17th 1901

My dear Gertie
You will think that Mary and I are very unkind not to have written and told you about all our gay doings down here in 'marvellous Melbourne'. I think our intentions were good, I know mine were but after the celebrations we were all pretty well tired out and there seemed to be so many people in the house that one never had time to spare for letter-writing. During the fortnight the Royal pair were our guests we were mostly out of the house from early morn till late at night, just coming home for meals when we could get on to a tram or when the crowds weren't too much for us. Everyone was glad when the time was over yet everyone acknowledges that it was all so lovely and enjoyable. You've had the Australasian so you will have some idea of how our streets were decorated and let me tell you that our streets are worth decorating. They are so wide and undulating I'm sure the Duke and Duchess never passed thro. seven miles of such beautiful roads in their life before. I think the day of their arrival must have been a great surprise to them, it must have given them a thrill of pride and pleasure to think that this beautiful city with its magnificent roads lined with dense crowds of cheering people belonged to them or would some day. On that day I took Mother into my brother's office which stands at the corner of William and Collins St. The procession came down William St into Collins St so that from our window we had a splendid view. The others had

all left very early in the morning to take up positions in various places. Mother and I left home about 11.30am and got into our places at 12 noon; there we had to wait till the procession passed at 3.30. On an ordinary occasion this waiting would have been tedious but there were troops moving about constantly down the streets taking up their positions. The troops were from all over Australia, Fiji and New Zealand and on this day lined the 7 mile route where the procession passed. In front of our window 2000 cadets were drawn up. Poor little chaps were on their feet from 9 o'clock till 3.30 and then they had to march back to Barracks. The officers let them sit down for a while and it was comical to see them spreading their handkerchiefs on the road before doing so. Then the crowd behind them passed through fruit and biscuits so that the kids did well. At our corner the Mounted Band of the NSW Lancers were stationed. This was very interesting as it is the only full Military Band that is mounted. It seemed very strange to see these men riding along each playing his different instrument. The leading man was playing two drums and so his hands being fully occupied he guided his horse by means of reins attached to his feet or stirrup irons, then the two officers ride each side of him. All the waiting time the crowds were most enthusiastic and as you may know enthusiasm is very infectious so that you felt like cheering all the time. Mother tried to restrain me but I believe when at last the Duke did come Mother let out a feeble cheer herself. You see as each different body of soldiers passed the crowd gave them some kind of a welcome. All except the Westralians who were dressed in very plain khaki and came after the crowd had grown tired of cheering and waiting; I felt so sorry for them that I put my head out far and waved my handkerchief cheering wildly. The Officer in command saw and understood for he turned his horse a little and saluted. Mother didn't know whether she should rebuke me or not. At last the word came out that the outriders had turned into William St., then there was a breathless three minutes when everyone was qui vive and their eyes glued to the place where they reckoned they'd see the royal carriage first. You heard the cheers rumbling along as each crowd was passed, and then they came. Oh how the handkerchiefs went and the cheers and the bands playing God Save The King! Oh it was glorious to be amongst it all! The Royal Pair looked to me to be a little astonished, a little shy as if they'd like to be out of it all. He saluted gravely without a smile. She was smiling ever so slightly but with the sweetest expression imaginable. You noticed how very blue his eyes were, and how very lovely her hair was. Then they were gone and everything seemed flat and uninteresting again. We waited till the crowd dispersed a little and then we sallied forth to get a tram. A trooper on a beautiful horse wished to escort us down the street but Mother would not trust his beautiful dancing steed. When we got to where we should get a tram not one to be had. The crowd had rushed to Flinders St. and crowded the tram so that they were not able to come up the hill to us. So Mother and I had to take a hansom driving home in state. When we got home we found tea proceeding and around the table seventeen people seated. Such a hubbub you never did hear, everyone speaking at once telling what they saw, and Father trying to find out what he was to carve for each and everyone, and Mary's silvery tones inquiring 'milk and sugar so and so?' Mother and I were of no consequence, but after a while got some much needed tea.

That night at 15 to 6pm, we all left our house in a

huge furniture van to view the illuminations. There were about 25 of us altogether and we had taken enough good things with us to last a week's camping out, and yet we did not seem to have too much. This night was reserved for carriages so the newspaper said. Really it meant that the trams would be stopped and the roadways kept clear to allow vehicles to pass in line through Melbourne. You could not break your line and you had to go and do what the police told you. So that there was a line of all sorts of carts buggies vans going one way and another going the other way from 5pm till 12am and after too. Some people never got into Melbourne at all after waiting hours and hours. We left our houses at 15 to 6 and got into Melbourne at 8.30 – 2 miles in over 2 hours, but the time seemed very short owing to the fun amongst ourselves and among the crowd. The police prevented us going down Bourke St. as the crowds had got so dense they could not manage them and we were sent home in a very round about way arriving at 10.30. Well thus ended the first day and when I tell you that was nearly the quietest day I had you will understand how we rushed the other days. Mary and I got beautiful black evening dresses for the affairs in the Exhibition for as you know Father got invites to all the Commonwealth Celebrations. Mary's dress is black sequin net over black satin, very prettily made and suits her perfectly. She has such a nice neck and arms for evening dress. Mine are very scraggy at present but the dressmaker did the best for me and you don't notice my salt cellars very much. My dress is, to give it its proper name, black mousseline de soie over black satin trimmed with white chiffon fichu and long chiffon sash from the shoulder. The only lady to compare with us in the way of dressing was the Duchess!! And then that was because she had such beautiful diamonds and we had none. At the Royal Concert I had a splendid view of the Ducal party and you may be sure I took them all in. The Duchess is very much taller than the Duke and her diamonds made her look even more stately. She was always of course dressed in black except for the white ribbon across her breast from her shoulder to her waist, it is some order or other. She conversed to Lord Hopetoun very naturally and the Countess entertained the Duke. Of course they only stayed an hour, arriving at 9.15. We arrived with the other 8000 guests at 7. o'clock. Everyone was determined to get good seats. Father looked splendid in his evening clothes, I really do believe he was quite the handsomest man there and I was very proud to be walking alongside him. There were at all these gatherings numbers of red-coated generals and admirals etc., making the place look very gay. Soldiers and naval men were very plentiful, so common that you soon forgot to look at them or ask whom they were. Are you sick of celebrations? Perhaps you are for the newspapers are full of all the doings of the Royal Pair. I must tell you though one more little incident just to show you what a nice couple they are. You know that when leaving Melbourne they drove through Albert Park, South Melbourne, and when passing through the two latter places they would have to pass through the poorest parts of Melbourne. Wide enough streets but such small houses with poor wretched people living in them. But nearly all these houses had hanging out some coloured paper or tiny flag or gaudy picture to mark their loyalty. Well to get to my story – in one of these streets three very dirty little boys were making mud pies in the gutter, no boots or stockings and you couldn't tell what garments they had on, perhaps one leg of their father's trousers between the lot of them.

Still they were healthy as gutter children often are and they were good specimens. Well just as the Royal carriage came up to 'the gutter trio' they jumped up and gave three lusty cheers, throwing their caps in the air. The Duchess noticed them and touched the Duke's arm to point them out to him, then she smilingly bowed three times to them, and the Duke saluted with a very broad smile. An awful dirty old woman near-by wished that she had been one of those boys to get that bow and smile. The going away was not attended by such crowds as previously as it was not a public holiday and the route was very long.

Now I think I had better leave royalty alone and come down to real life. How are you getting on without Jack? Glad to have a little time to yourself I suspect. He must be such a bother to have to entertain. I hope you are all well. We are having such frightfully cold weather, dull and raining. I suppose Jack is having a bad time poor chap. Such a long drought and now floods. Some things are hard to understand, but every cloud has a silver lining.

Now I will read over your letter and see if there are any questions to answer. I am afraid you treated that cousin of yours in a very unkind manner, or he wouldn't have been so afraid of your laughter.
Do I remember Mr McMahon? I wasn't much of a rider but his riding nearly killed me and the others always left me to take care of him. I was glad to see the last of him. I don't know whether I ever told Jack but he used to be always writing poetry to me. I was horribly ashamed as if it was my fault and kept the fact hidden. I've still a piece left which I would send you if I knew exactly where to find it. He had a very rough time that visit, I was always staying in my room all day if the others left him at home or sneeking out on lonely excursions by myself. I'm glad for the

horses that he rides a bike. I don't mind so much being in the house by myself for a bit, and last time I was very glad as I was not feeling as sweet tempered as I might have been. I had the blues – ever had them? Aren't they horrid? Of course the housemaid who was with me was a jewel and then generally someone came in to see very often. You speak of Mr Aitken. Didn't he call one evening at Rawbelle when I was all alone? I only saw him for a moment or two but thought he was very nice. Is he engaged that you speak of him marrying? Have you still that very entertaining young clergyman who visited Rawbelle once while I was there? He was a specimen. Now I must stop. Things are humdrum here now. I have been for a change for two weeks and feel much better and a little fatter. Went to the tennis dance the other night just to show my new dress off and to my surprise enjoyed myself. Give my love to Mrs Hindmarsh – I don't forget her kindness to me yet never shall. Remember me to Mr Hindmarsh and Gavin if he is still at Rawbelle. And with much love to you.

I remain
Yours affectionately
Ethel Shaw

P.S. I wish you would formally introduce your sister to me. I feel as if I know her quite well and often want to send her a message or even write her a letter, but I doubt if she would think I was proper if I did so without an introduction. Ask her if she will become acquainted with me. Does Burnie remember me?

E.G.S.

The headmaster of a two-teacher school in Renmark, South Australia, OTTHO GOLDSWORTHY, *wrote this quaint letter to Mr Philpot (not Philpott as written), the father of one of his pupils, Ivy Philpot (pictured), in 1915 after learning that Ivy would be leaving school to to commence her career of 'helping mother'. This letter was provided by Ivy's son, Rex Hobcroft, of Melville, Perth.*

PUBLIC SCHOOL
RENMARK WEST
Dec. 14th, 15

Dear Sir,

Ivy informed me today that she was commencing her career of 'helping mother'.

It has always been a great pleasure to have her as a pupil, she has been quite a model in work, appearance and conduct, and I feel sure she will reflect as much credit on you later as she does now.

With best wishes to Mrs Philpott and yourself for Christmas season.

Your sincerely,
Ottho E. Goldsworthy

DORIS GARRET, *15, and her father, a superintendent at Cockatoo Island Dock, had been travelling home to Vaucluse in Sydney on the ferry* Greycliffe *when it collided with a US mail steamer, the* Tahiti. *The wooden ferry, crossing from Circular Quay to Watsons Bay, was torn in half and in the dusk chaos 40 people drowned. At the time, people were relieved the death toll wasn't higher as dozens of school children had been on board after attending the Public Schools Amateur Athletic Association Games. This letter was written by Doris on 9 November; the accident occurred on 3 November. It is addressed to Mrs Hammond and her four-year-old son, Ian, who had moved to England. Doris had been Ian's babysitter. Ian de Lisle Hammond, who now lives at Nowra in NSW and is 78, still has the letter but lost touch with Doris after she and her mother moved to Melbourne in 1938.*

1927
NOVEMBER 9
VAUCLUSE, NSW

Dear Mrs Hammond and Ian,

Only bad news to tell you this time. Perhaps you have already heard about the terrible ferry accident but as it happened it was the 4.15 from town which Dad and I catch every day. You will see from this letter that I am quite safe but they haven't found Dad yet.

Coming home as usual on Thursday we were watching the Tahiti, one of the Union line steamers, coming down the harbour; it seemed closer than usual but we enjoyed it, then as we neared Bradley's Head both boats seemed to swerve and we were hurried round the other side. The bump was awful, the water pushed up behind a seat which knocked me into the water, I was about the first in. I thought of Dad but couldn't reach him. In the water I was turned over and over by the force of the propellors from the big boat and the suction dragged everybody down. I worked my legs trying to get up quicker but was soon exhausted and just let myself go. I seemed to be going deeper and deeper judging by the colour of the water. Still I didn't open my mouth or swallow any water. When I came to the top I was by myself and was too weak to stay up so I went down again.

The next time I came up I saw two boys and a girl sitting on a floating seat. They couldn't help me but one boy called out to me and encouraged me to get to them. How I did it I don't know but I got to the raft and could just manage to keep my head out of the water. My legs were getting cramped and all I could think of was Dad. After being in the water about 10 minutes a little tug came along and threw out two lifebelts. I didn't get one so I determined not to be alone and climbed up the side of the boat. Once on the boat I let go of my feelings and screamed out for Dad.

The boys were really wonderful right through. They even took off their wet coats and put them round us. Well they took us into Sydney to see who should go to the hospital. They asked me to go but I came home to Mum. About six reporters interviewed us, took our photos etc.

Then they were kind enough to bring us home. When I arrived home only to find that Dad was not there I think I could have died. I only got one bruise where the seat knocked me over. I lost my bag full of books, purse, new hat and Dad. The drivers are busy raising the boat and seeing if there is anybody buried in the sand. I hope they find Dad. The people have been so good and although we hadn't made many friends they have been in ever since Thursday. We received some lovely letters from the Island about Dad and I am trying to answer as many as I can. I think more people have been killed and injured down our street than anywhere else. I can remember about four dead and 14 injured.

Do you remember Dora Hill, my friend, well her little sister Agnes was drowned. I have been to see as many people as I was able to and most of the women who have lost anyone are nearly frantic but Mum is bearing up well. She hasn't slept much but I have slept more than usual I think.

Oh, Mr Hammond called and offered his sympathies to Mum and offered to do anything she wanted. He has been at the morgue all the time waiting to see Dad, he said he wouldn't go till he saw him and he also said that Dad was one of the finest men that ever walked on this earth! I thought it was a wonderful thing to say. Betty Sharp, Mrs Hodgson's daughter, is still missing.

On the Thursday night after the accident I had two reporters in to see me and they got the whole story from me and the next morning it was in the paper with a few additions to it. The man next door but one to us is pretty bad and is worrying because he didn't save anybody, I think he had a pretty hard job to save himself. Last night Dad's boss from the Island came with his wife and he was unable to speak except for an occasional word here and there but he couldn't speak highly enough of Dad and how valuable he was.

But this is enough of this mournful stuff and I hope you will write to us from time to time and forgive Mum for not writing but she has had a funny feeling for the last three months. I wish we could have a good talk and I'd love to see Ian, perhaps I will some day.

With love to you both from us both
Doris

CHARLES KINNE *(pictured) was the quintessential Australian country school teacher. He taught thousands of Queensland students in a career spanning nearly fifty years, and spent many hundreds of hours tutoring pupils out of school hours who were struggling with their work. Among his earlier students were the Johnston twins of Kingaroy, two teenage brothers he tutored just before he set off on his own to work at a series of one-teacher schools in rural Queensland. According to a note Mr Kinne added to this letter from the twins' mother, Lannie Johnston, the brothers were both shot down and killed during World War II. Mr Kinne spent many years in Queensland until his retirement, when he moved to Tasmania to live with one of his two daughters. He died in 1992, aged 83. This letter was contributed by Mr Kinne's youngest daughter, Cynthia Spratt of Blackmans Bay, Tasmania.*

1935
OCTOBER
KINGAROY

Dear Mr Kenney [Kinne],

Thank you very much indeed for all the extra time you are spending to help the boys along. I think you are just splendid and we appreciate it very highly. And you seem to be bringing them along far better than ever I expected. They lost over 12 months moving about. Please axcept [sic] cake for morning tea and if you have any 'specials' please send along and I will make it for you. A China cup and saucer of mine somewhere at school since cricket if you can locate, and needing one, you can keep for self. Also, if you would care for afternoon tea at school I have small set complete will only be too pleased to send along with milk etc and think it a pleasure to do so thanking you once again.

From sincerely yours
Lannie E. Johnston

P.S. I wanted to write and send a note of thanks months ago but twins shy re cakes, notes etc.

In 1884, MARGARET HARRISON, *an Aboriginal woman living on the Ebenezer Mission Station near Dimboola in Victoria, learned of the death of one of her three daughters, Edith Taylor. Her daughters were living on the Lake Condah Aboriginal Reserve near Hamilton in the Western District of Victoria. She wrote this moving letter to Captain Page, Inspector to the Central Board for the Protection of Aborigines, to ask for the return of her other two daughters. Her plea was granted. This letter is held by the National Archives of Australia (Melbourne) (CRS B 313/122). A landmark book produced by the Australian Archives and Public Record Office Victoria,* My Heart Is Breaking *(AGPS, 1993), was named in honour of this letter.*

9 April 1884

Dear Sir

Please would you kindly allow me to have my two girls with me here as one of them died & I have not seen her before she died and I should like the other two to be with me to comfort me.

Please do not disapoint me for my heart is breaking to have them with me. Please to send them up here as I cannot leave this Station.

Please to ask Mr Stahle to let them come.

I am your obedient servant
Margaret Harrison
P.S. Let me know

WILLIAM *and* MARY BRAY *knew their world was changing in 1941, and that their twelve children would be dramatically affected. The Bray children were removed from their home to a place called the Bungalow. Mary Bray worked there as a cleaner and so had regular contact with her children, but she was prevented from talking to them in her language or teaching them her culture. This letter is held by the National Archives of Australia in Darwin, and was published in* Between Two Worlds *(IAD Press, 1995). It is published with permission from a granddaughter of William and Mary Bray, Leonie Bray, who lives in Alice Springs.*

1941
APRIL
NORTHERN TERRITORY
TO PROTECTOR OF ABORIGINALS

Dear Sir,

I myself, and my wife, both half castes we understand, do not want any of our children removed, out of this Central Australia their country.

It would not be fair to us, the loss of them. Also not fair to them, the loss of their parents, causing crying and fretting. We parents, born Arltunga Goldfields, children also, except one, he being the eldest – Norman. He born Deep Well, part of the east-west running James Range.

As we were all born here in Central Australia, we don't know any other parts, and don't want to.

Will you please place this Protest, as we do not understand any forcible removal, of any of us, from this Central Australia, our birthright country.

Yours truly
W. Bray

JOHN VAUTIN *(pictured) wrote this letter to the editor of* The Australian *newspaper in February 1998 during the sitting of Australia's Constitutional Convention in Old Parliament House, Canberra. The convention was held to determine whether the nation should become a republic. A model for a republic could not be agreed upon, and so the verdict of the convention was that we shouldn't become a republic. Vautin, who served in the Royal Australian Infantry with 4th Battalion in Borneo and 9th Battalion in Vietnam, and who was Mentioned in Dispatches for bravery, is a royalist but believes it is up to the young people of today to determine Australia's future. He has two adult children, Robert, 35, and Drew, 30, and two grandchildren. He and his wife, Robyn, who submitted this letter, retired to Coolum on the Sunshine Coast in Queensland in 1994.*

February 10, 1998

Dear Editor

Probably due to my age, I am a monarchist. Unquestionably my military service encouraged this state of mind. A consequence of this service was that I was at the local celebration of the ceremony celebrating the 75th anniversary of Anzac. I was passed a flame symbolically passing on the spirit of Anzac. It may sound naive, but it was serious and seriously emotional. I shed tears, and, ashamed, hid them from contemporaries.

I have been viewing the people's convention on ABC television. I am impressed enormously, not by the 'big end of town', but by the sincerity, intellect and lucidity of the young speakers. I remember less of what they espoused than of their images. I recall a beautiful young woman who appeared to be Eurasian in background. I recall an earnest bespectacled young man, a lady with outrageous hair and so many others.

I don't really agree with any of them, but they are young, they are beautiful and they are Australian. They are exactly the reason, indeed, the core of the rationale, that impelled me to forsake hearth and home and bear arms to distant lands in the name of 'democracy'.

I wish to pass the flame to them. I have absolute confidence that they will get it right. Anyway, the flame is burning my fingers.

I hope they tell Mr Turnbull and all the big end of town to 'go to buggery', or some other place equally favoured in Aussie vernacular.

I don't know who Bruce Ruxton served with, but I was infantry, and fought, I thought, for democracy. Go for it, young Australia. I'll explain it to the boys who died for king and country when I have my annual chat at first light on April 25.

John Vautin,
Coolum Beach, Qld

Letters from the Front

JOHN MONASH, *in 1915 commander of the 4th Infantry Brigade of the AIF, wrote this letter to his wife, Hannah, the night before the Anzac landing at Gallipoli. Within 24 hours, 2000 of his men would be dead. By the end of the campaign nine months later, 8709 Australian soldiers would have lost their lives. Despite this devastating defeat, John Monash (pictured with his wife Hannah and daughter Bertha) went on to be considered Australia's finest wartime general. He was promoted to Brigadier-General and led Australian troops on the Western Front. He was awarded a knighthood in 1917 and his face features on the $100 note. This letter is held by the Australian War Memorial.*

TRANSPORT A.31
SEEANGCHOON
April 24/15

Dearest Wife,

We have received our sailing orders, and inside of a few hours shall be in the thick of the greatest combined naval and military operation in history, with Australia in the pride of place. – That we shall succeed I do not entertain any doubt, but that I shall come through unscathed and alive is not so certain. – As this may be the last opportunity I have of talking to you, I want to say briefly that, in the event of my going out, you are to believe that I do so with only one regret, which is, the grief that this will bring to you and Bert and Mat. – For myself, I am prepared to take my chance. – While, on the one hand, to win through safely would mean honour and achievement, on the other hand to fall would mean an honorable end. – At best I have only a few years of vigour left, and then would come decay and the chill of old age, & perhaps lingering illness. – So, with the full and active life I have had, I need not regard the prospect of a sudden end with dismay. – I am greatly comforted to know that you will be well provided for, and will be surrounded by many friends, who, for my sake, will help you to win through all difficulties that may beset you in the future. – I am sure you know how deeply I have always loved you, and how in all things I have tried to act in your best interests. – I know also that you have loved me dearly, and will honor my memory.

Your husband
John Monash

DAVID GORDON *(pictured with his sons, John on the right and Douglas) wrote this letter to his son and 'mate' John on the eve of his son's departure to World War I. John fought in the ill-fated Gallipoli campaign, but was sent home after five months with chronic dysentery. He was one of the few survivors of the 10th Battalion. He later rejoined the war with the Royal Flying Corps, and went on to win an MC in France. After his return to Australia, John, among other things, worked for the fledgling Holden company in Adelaide. In 1924 he married Marjorie Murphy, and the couple had four children: Heather, Lyn, Richard and Bruce. It is Bruce Gordon of Willunga, South Australia, who is the holder of this, the only surviving letter from his grandfather to his father. John, who also served in the RAAF from 1939 to 1945, and Marjorie had been married 54 years when John died in 1978.*

1914
SEPTEMBER 28
(Your mother's birthday)
UNLEY PARK, SOUTH AUSTRALIA

My dear 'Mate',

You are about to leave the shelter of your home for foreign parts in the service of your King against the enemies of the Empire. This momentous step is your own deliberate choice springing spontaneously from your conception of duty. I want to assure you that your decision has the unqualified approval of your mother, myself, and your sisters. Your resolve to wear the King's uniform sprang from a desire to accept the obligations of manhood as well as that of citizenship, and of our great Commonwealth which is part of our

greater Empire. A man can have no purpose more noble than to offer his life as a sacrifice to a righteous cause in the service of his country. Your ancestors counted no sacrifice too great to win for you the liberties you have enjoyed in this fair land and you would have been unworthy of the British stock from which you came had you turned a deaf ear to the urgent appeal for help which came over the seas from our kinsfolk. We are proud of you, proud of you for all you have been and for all you have stood for, proud of you for having voluntarily exchanged the comforts and safety of your home for all the hardships of a soldier's life and the dangers inevitably associated with a campaign in foreign lands against a powerful and unscrupulous foe. England's cause is Australia's cause. We have shared her triumphs and gloried in her traditions and cowards we would have been had we stood idly by – deaf to her entreaties and blind to the grim struggle in which our countrymen are engaged for the honour of the empire and for all that civilisation means. No, my dear boy, we do not ask you to stay in safety at home far removed from the tumult of battle.

Go forward, and be helped in your high resolve not only by our parting cheers, sustained not only by our prayers, but comforted in the lonely vigils of a soldier's duty with the knowledge that your conception of duty and ours is the same.

Even if I could trust myself to pen the thoughts that come flooding upon me I would hesitate to say more than that your mother and I have absolute confidence that you will do your duty as a soldier and a man. You have never once given us cause to doubt your courage or question your fidelity. We, for our part, have sought to guide you by example. We have encouraged you to exercise your free will and allow your own conscience to govern your actions and this appeal to your better nature during boyhood, and manhood has never been in vain.

The memory of your home and all it stands for; of your parents and your sisters; the honour of the family; your 'active service' for King and Country; your own faith in the Divine Power; will, we know, strengthen and sustain you in the midst of temptations, hardships and perils. On the field of sport you have always 'played the game' and you have played it like a true sportsman.

'Play the game', my dear 'mate', all the time in all circumstances, in every condition, remembering

'To set the cause above renown
To love the game beyond the prize
To honour, while you strike him down
The foe with fearless eyes.'

Good-bye my dear old boy – always and forever my 'mate'. May providence be with you, watch over and direct you; Temperance in all things chasten you; Fortitude support you; and Justice be the guide of all your actions. 'God bless and keep you safe' will always be the prayer.

Your loving mate and dad

HUGH THOMAS (TOM) SHAW *left school at the age of eleven, yet achieved sufficient command over the English language to pen this marvellously evocative letter about the sights and sounds of exotic Cairo in 1915. It was at the very start of World War I and Tom was writing to his sister-in-law Rachael (Ray) Shaw. He had already served with the 1st West Australian Mounted Infantry in South Africa during the Boer War and re-enlisted, at the age of 40, with the 11th Battalion AIF for World War I. After writing this letter, he was sent to Gallipoli, after which he was deemed medically unfit for active service. Tom went on to live to the age of 90 in his much loved town of Bunbury in Western Australia, where he became foundation member of the Bunbury RSL in 1917. He had seven brothers, four of whom served in – and survived – the Boer War and three of whom served in and survived World War I. Tom went on to have five children with his wife May. This letter is contributed by a grandson of Tom Shaw, Bill Thomas of Elanora on the Gold Coast.*

My address is
Sergt Tom Shaw
HEADQUARTERS
11TH BATTLN
3RD INF BRIGADE
A.I.E.F.
EGYPT
Jan 9th 1915

Dear Ray
I got your very welcome letter on Xmas day also one from May, No Xmas box could have been more acceptable. I bet that when you wrote it you did not think I would be reading it on Xmas day almost in the shadow of the great Pyramids. No words of mine can tell you of the wonders of this place, and yet here am I one unit of a great wonder. Just imagine yourself in a great city of canvas with sand hills all around and on those sand hills here and there, all over the place, men drawn up in hollow squares about 1000 men in each, then listen and from one square rises Nearer my God to Thee, from another Onward Christian Soldiers, another further on, Jesus Lover of my Soul and so on right round the camp each Battalion on its own Church Parade ground (There are three Brigades of twelve battalions in each Bgde) and looking down on all, the great pyramids built at least 2500 years before Christ was born, no doubt they have seen many curious sights throughout the centuries but surely this is one of the strangest, Australian troops with their bands singing the praises of their God before the monuments of men who in their little

way thought that they themselves were gods. Every Sunday this wonder is enacted and when I am there with the other men I cannot help feeling that I am a small thing indeed a speck in the great scheme of things, more infinite than the tiniest grain of sand that I crush beneath my feet as I march to and from the Parade ground. It is a sermon in itself to stand before these monuments of man's vanity and think of the few short hours the men who built them had to live and love and enjoy their short span of life, short in comparison even to the life of their own memorials yet how much shorter in comparison to the Eternal, well Ray you will think that I have got 'em, but I am only trying to put into words what I feel. This is a strange land, Cairo is a beautiful city, yet Cairo is like a beautiful woman whose beauty is skin deep, and whose outer garments are pure and white while underneath her garments are soiled & filthy. In all directions rise Mosques whose minarets point to the sky the delicate carving of the tiers of balconies making them look like cuffs of lace. Churches of all shade of Christian thought R.C., C. of E., Greek Orthodox, Coptic, all having their own particular style of beauty. Palaces fit for any King, beautiful hotels, and amidst all hovels worse than dog kennels, poverty, filth, and squalor to sicken anyone. Women are as cattle, treated a little better maybe because they give their masters more pleasure, and incidentally propagate the species. All nations are mixed here and the vilest of the Mediteranean [sic] seem to dominate. According to an official statement just lately made there are 80,000 immoral women in Cairo, 30,000 of whom are licensed by the Govt to carry on their trade, the other 50,000 are a menace to the health of the community. At present there are about 70,000 troops camped in and around Cairo, so you can just imagine what things are like, the hospitals are full, and you can take it from me that for every 100 men who are invalided from here (either to Australia or elsewhere) there are 99 who are victims of their own folly and the filthy state of these women.

They are of all nations black white brown and yellow, but no English or American woman is allowed to remain, that is seen to by the English officials and it helps to keep up the prestige of the English speaking races. Another contrast in Cairo is the age old Nile and the most modern bridges, the electric trams running right to the Pyramids past oriental palaces with the barred windows of the Harems showing where some big pot has his women caged up. And the road from Cairo to the Pyramids (about 12 miles) is another wonder in itself, one can bowl along in a splendid up to date motor car and on the same road are trams donkeys camels buffaloes goats horses etc. such a medley, and right alongside of the road you see a miserable specimen of a man plowing with two buffaloes and a couple of pieces of stick fixed just exactly the same as the Egyptians used before the Pyramids were built. Well Ray old girl I will not weary you with any more descriptions of the things I have seen. I will try to write a few things for the Paper later on and so will be able to give all a glimpse of Egypt through my eyes.

Sep is looking well and I am feeling ditto, though there is a lot of sickness, apart from what I have mentioned nearly everyone has a cold and many influenza etc. I hope Charlie stays at home.

Love to Wally & Marta Charlie & yourself from Tom.

It takes just a few minutes to read through MARY ANN DRUMMOND*'s efforts to locate her son, Victor Emanuel Farr, in the aftermath of Gallipoli. But glance at the dates atop each one in this series of letters, and you begin to realise the ongoing anguish with which this grieving mother was destined to live. For years she battled bureaucracies and the tyranny of distance to learn anything about the fate of her son Victor Farr. It was a full six years before she learned officially that her boy was dead – and even then there was no word about where he was buried. And nor was there ever to be. Twenty years after Victor Farr last wrote to his mother from the war front, the official word finally came through. He was killed in action at Gallipoli. His body was never recovered, and he has no known grave. These letters are held by the National Archives of Australia in Canberra (B2455: Personal dossiers of members of the 1st AIF; Farr V. E. 828).*

AUGUST 4, 1915
Base Records Office, AIEF
TO MRS M. DRUMMOND,
CATHERINE HILL BAY, NSW

Dear Madam,

In reply to your enquiry of the 30th ult, concerning your son, No. 828 Private V.E. Farr, 1st Battalion, I beg to inform you he is not reported as seriously wounded, and Egypt advises in the absence of further reports, it is to be assumed all wounded are progressing satisfactorily.

It is regretted that the nature of his wound and the hospital in which he is located are at present unknown. Next-of-kin will be immediately notified upon receipt of any further information.

His postal address is as follows: No. 828 Private V. E. Farr, Wounded, 1st Battalion, lst Infantry Brigade, 1st Australian Division, Alexandria, Egypt.

Yours faithfully,
Capt. Officer i/c Base Records

AUGUST 23, 1915
Catherine Hill Bay, NSW
TO THE SECRETARY OF DEFENCE

Dear Sir,

I received a cablegram on 15th June stating my son V.E. Farr was wounded and since then although making inquiries in both Sydney and Melbourne, I have been unable to find out the nature of his wound or locate the Hospital in which he is in and it is now 10 weeks since I first got a cable stating he was wounded. I may state a young man that left here with my son at the break out of war. He is a Copr in 2 Batt writing to a friend of mine and in his letter which he received on the 20th of this month he states that the first account he got of my son was that he was wounded but a later account he got was that he was missing. Now Sir, I think it is your duty to see or have this seen to for me. I think when a mother gives her son, seeing that he is under age when that son is wounded she ought to have some news of the nature of his wound or the hospital in which he is in. It is now 10 weeks I think they have had ample time to let me know something of my son.

Dear Sir I also ask you seeing that I live 22 miles out from Newcastle and work being very slack I expect you to cable for information for me and oblige me with an early reply. Hoping that I am not asking too much but I think I should know where my son is and I do hope you will give me the information which I am waiting anxiously for day after day.

I remain yours sincerely,
Mrs M. Drummond

SEPTEMBER 10, 1915
Catherine Hill Bay, NSW
TO BASE RECORDS OFFICE, MELBOURNE

Dear Sir,

Yours to hand today and was very much disappointed to learn that you could not supply me with any information in respect to my son Private V.E. Farr. Well, sir this is the address of the young man that said he was reported missing in the trenches: 647 Corp T Mathers, MG Section 2nd Batt, AIF M.E.F. Hoping this will receive attention and that you will be able to furnish me with some reliable information as soon as possible.

I remain yours etc
Mrs M Drummond.

P.S. It is almost 15 weeks since I received a cable saying he was wounded. It is very odd that I have had no word from him before this as he used to write so regular. Before this, the last letter I received from him was written on April 24.

OCTOBER 6, 1915
Catherine Hill Bay, NSW
TO MR MATT CHARLTON, MEMBER, NORTH LAMBTON, NSW

Dear Sir,

I hope you will excuse me writing to you as I have been advised to do. I am very anxious about my son who has been fighting at the Dardanelles and was reported wounded 15 June last and we cannot get any tidings of him. I have written to the Defence Department in Melbourne but they say they don't know where he is or where he was taken to when wounded. Sir I don't know if you can do anything to find out where my son is, if he is living or not if you have a son at the front you will have an idea what it is like to wait for months for news it is very trying indeed. I am sending an addressed stamped envelope if you would be kind enough to write a few lines and tell me if you will be able to find out anything. This is my boy's address: No. 828 pte. V.E. Farr, D Company, 1st Battalion, 1st Infantry Brigade, 1st Australian Division, Alexandria, Egypt.

I remain yours obediently,
Mary Drummond

NOVEMBER 5, 1915
CAIRO, TO 1ST AIF

Witness said that Farr was missed on the first day and that nothing was heard of him. He added that he did not see how it was possible for anything definite to be known about Farr or others lost on the first day. Witness Ref: Pte A. Bone, 704, 1 AIF C Coy. 5th Training Battalion, Zeitoun

W.H.V. Reade

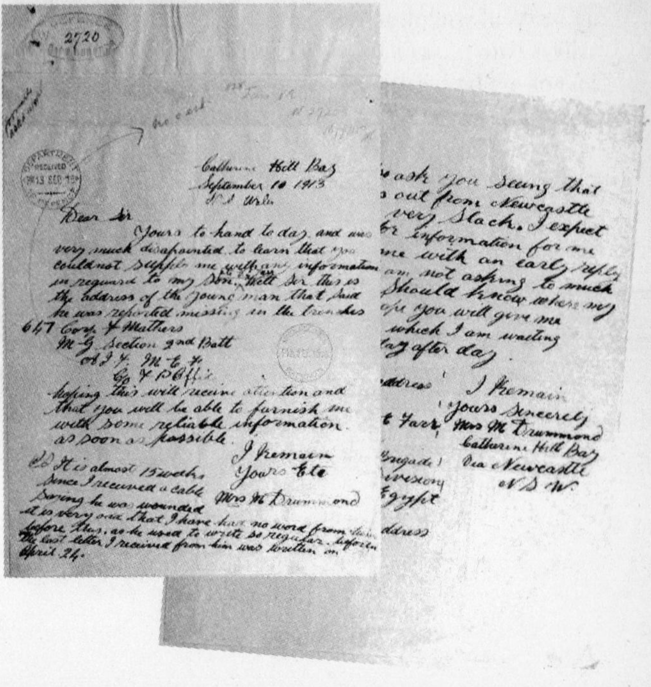

2720

Catherine Hill Bay
September 10 1915
N S Wales

Dear Sir

Yours to hand to day and was very much disapointed to learn that you couldnot supply me with any information in regaurd to my Son. Well Sir this is the address of the young man that said he was reported missing in the trenches

647 Corp. F Mathers
M-G Section 2nd Batt
A I F. M-E F.
G P O

hoping this will receive attention and that you will be able to furnish me with some reliable information as soon as possible.

I remain
Yours Etc
Mrs M Drummond

PS It is almost 15 weeks since I received a cable saying he was wounded it is very odd that I have had no word from him before this, as he used to write so regular. before the last letter I received from him was written on April 24.

…ask you seeing that
…out from Newcastle
…very slack. I expect
…or information for me
…me with an early reply
…am not asking to much
…should know where my
…ope you will give me
…which I am waiting
…day after day.

…ddress

I remain
Yours sincerely
Mrs M Drummond
Catherine Hill Bay
Via Newcastle
N S W.

…t Farr,
…rigade
…ivision
…Egypt
…ddress

MAY 14, 1921
Cessnock, NSW
TO THE OFFICER IN CHARGE
BASE RECORDS,
VICTORIA BARRACKS,
MELBOURNE

Dear Sir,

Your letter to hand yesterday referring to my poor boy's place of burial. I only wish you could tell me if you knew he was buried, my sorrow would not be so great but no one can tell me if he was wounded and missing from the day of the Gallipoli landing later reported killed on that day. Enclosed you will find letters I received from his mate. They may assist. Will you please return them. Trusting you will excuse me as I am very much worried at the loss of my boy.

I remain yours sincerely
Mary Drummond

SEPTEMBER 23, 1935
Office of Base Records, Sydney
TO OFFICER IN CHARGE BASE RECORDS, VICTORIA BARRACKS, MELBOURNE

Dear Sir,

I have to acknowledge receipt of your communication of 19.9.1935 relative to the affairs of the late No. 828 Private Victor E. Farr, 1st Battalion, and in reply to inform you with regret that according to the records this soldier was reported Killed in Action at Gallipoli between the 25th and 29th April, 1915. Unfortunately, despite the most searching enquiry and investigation, the Imperial War Graves Commission have not been successful in recovering the remains of the late Private Farr; and, in common with those of other of his comrades who fell at Gallipoli and have no known graves, his name has been commemorated on the Lone Pine Memorial to the Missing.

Yours faithfully,
T. Robinson, Officer i/c Base Records, Sydney

This letter was found in TOM GARD'S *wallet after he was killed by German shellfire while marching to the front near Paschendale, Belgium, on 6 August 1916. A slight man, he felt compelled to enlist after receiving a white feather in the mail, and was among the first Australians aboard ships to Europe. He was twenty years old when he died. The writer, Edna Wood (the sketch overleaf of whom was also found in Tom's wallet), was born in Western Australia in 1900. She went on to marry James Henry Lees in 1920, dying tragically in Red Cliffs, Victoria, at the age of 28, shortly after the birth of her second son. This letter was contributed by a nephew of Tom, Clive Gard of St Ives in Sydney.*

With Love

From Edna

30/3/16

1916
JUNE 1
KALGOORLIE

My darling Tom,

I received your letter love and I was so very pleased to get it. I didn't expect it so it was much nicer. I had such a nice letter from your father and Elsie and they want me to go down to your place. I would like to very much. I don't know if I told you or not – that I'm working now – I'm bookkeeping and typewriting in the largest accountants and auditors office in Kalgoorlie – so love you can guess I've got plenty to do – and I can't find a minute to spare to write to anyone. I start work at nine and finish at six. I've got a lovely boss – he rather spoils me a bit – he lets me know when I'm working too hard and lets me know when I'm sitting in a draught. He's just like a Father to me. I had a letter from Mrs Row – she wants to come up to Kalgoorlie too – since I told her that we haven't had any rain for months. The camp has closed down at Bunbury owing to the terrible damp weather that they are having down there. It's just as well I'm out of it between the quietness and the wet weather – it wouldn't be too pleasant. I'm so glad to hear you had a nice trip over to Egypt and good food not very often they get good food. My Brother is in

France – as I suppose you know. Our 'Baby' is still in the Sanatorium and I hope he stops there.

I went to the Dandies last night and had a lovely time – I went especially to see the chap Throssell VC. I suppose you have heard of him getting the VC. He's from Northam. He has been practically all over the world since he enlisted and returned back here.

My darling Tom – did you get all my letters when you arrived in Egypt? I hope you did love. I'm always waiting for the Egyptian mail to see if I could get a letter from you. So darling be sure and write to me. Remember your promise when you said Goodbye to me love. Well darling love I must close as I'm so tired – eight o'clock is early rising for me. If I was home I wouldn't have much to do as we have a French maid now – she's very nice – she speaks broken English. Now my darling Goodnight, write next mail. With fondest love and heaps of kisses.

I remain ever your loving sweetheart
Edna. xxxxxxx.

DENE FRY *wrote this letter home to his mother, Caroline, after his brother Alan was killed in action on the Western Front at twenty-one. Dene, who had been studying science at Sydney University when he enlisted, was killed less than twelve months later at Hermies. He was twenty-four. Dene and Alan had grown up the best of mates and it was only natural that Alan should follow his big brother into the AIF. A third brother, James Rollo, was shot down and killed over Holland in World War II. Their mother, Caroline, who had studied arts at Sydney University in the 1880s, died in 1954. This letter and photograph of Alan and Dene were recently featured in an exhibition at the State Library of NSW, 'Private Lives: Families of NSW'. They are reproduced with the permission of the Mitchell Library, State Library of NSW (ML MSS 6756) and Mrs Jean Fry of Burwood, Melbourne, the widow of James Rollo.*

BOVINGTON CAMP
WEST CAMP AIF
DORSET, ENG.
October 17, 1916

My Dear Mother,

I am far too upset and sick at heart to say much Mother dear, for I have just had a telegram from Tommy which tells me Alan died of wounds in France on August fourteenth. I can find no one who knew him intimately round about and so I have to just think of him and turn my sad thoughts over and over in my own mind. Everyone is very sympathetic and some of the returned boys have said some fine things which only those who have been through this hell can say. But we are far from anywhere here and the very locality and weather are cold and cheerless, and I admit I'm down.

Well Mother, as you know your son was not only my brother but my very best friend. I don't know of anyone who could ever say one word against him and I'm sure he never made an enemy. The Burns Philp boys will be dreadfully sorry and all the north shore line lads will I'm sure miss him. It leaves a great blank in my life which only little Bill's growing up can fill. I hope Hazel and Dorothy fully realise what Alan has sacrificed, and how they should cherish for ever all the kindest thoughts and remembrances of him, and remember that the greatest of all honours are his. All the world might stand and say – 'This was a man'. He had Uncle Fred's nature but said as little of his own troubles as did Uncle Jim. Believe me Mother dear, the people in Australia are sadly ignorant of things. But it is best so. The privations of Egypt even, which are sneered at if a man has not been to the front, and which Alan had so much of, were hardly mentioned by him. We have 1000 wounded men here from the Pozières action and all agree that Gallipoli was a mere picnic. France is a battle of mammoth engines and until the people realise we must have men, it will go on in the same equal way.

It's awfully hard to write about Alan. I'm thinking hard of him all the time but your pen can't go fast enough for your thoughts. Tommy has written me a beautiful letter, but I feel oh so lonely through it all, so much on my own, and not an old pal who knew him near me. I could get so much off my chest if I could only chat over his memory with an old pal. I cannot simply cannot say more Mother, you must just all picture me of hope and joy and fortune destitute, and turning it over and over in my tired mind. Father will be ever so proud, and so he should be. He can hold his head as high as the highest, for he is the father of a hero who has done his bit in this crisis. How can the women have anything to do with the boys at home? If everyone would only come forward it would all be over and done with. Birdwood wants 40,000 Australians & he is going to take Lil[l]e. There are no soldiers like them. Anzacs, especially these lame and sad-faced lads all around us, are the pride of the empire. They have acquitted themselves magnificently and paid a cruel price. I feel proud beyond words of Alan – just as proud as I felt when I knew dear little Marion was to be all mine.

The question of whether I should go to the front now that Alan has gone must only be solved in one way Mother dear. I will go. Don't worry over it. You know I was born lucky. There is not much chance of us being moved over to France for months. I don't think I will alter my mind, and even if I wanted it, I probably could not get a transfer. If conscription comes in it might make a difference. I will give it every consideration.

Give my best love to all at home. We have indeed suffered a sad sad thing in our happy home but it is a glorious thing. Goodbye Mother dear.

Your loving son
Dene

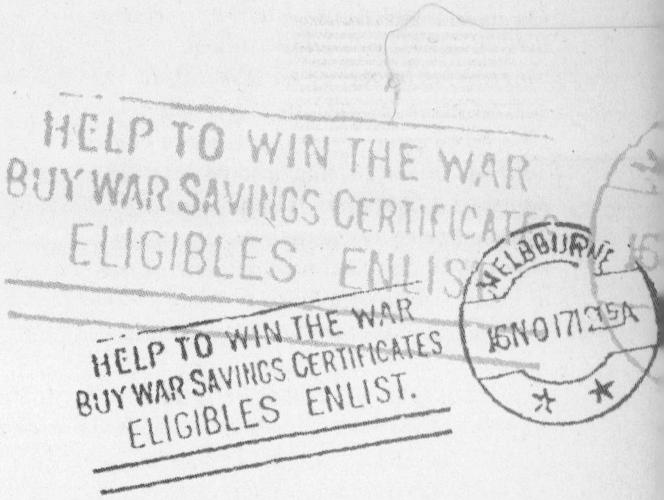

Australian soldiers became famous in World War I for having a tender side to their bravery. This letter was written by JULIAN E. McGUIRE, *serving on the front in France, to his namesake, Julian Thomas McGuire, who had just been born back in Adelaide. Although they shared a surname, they were not related. Julian E. was engaged to baby Julian's cousin, Ethel. The couple, who had been prevented from marrying during the war by Ethel's father, who did not want his daughter to become a war bride, were named as godparents to the young Julian. Sadly, the two Julians never met. Julian E. (pictured) was killed just before the war ended. Three of his brothers were also killed.*

Ethel never married, and lived out her days in Adelaide, dying thirteen years ago aged 89. Julian Thomas, who grew up to become a soldier himself and served in Darwin during World War II, also never married. What remains of the letter, some of which is now illegible, was found among his belongings in Adelaide when he died in 1999, aged 82. Also found was a silver spoon still in its original box and dated 'Christmas 1917 In the Field to the Baby'. Julian Thomas had never mentioned the spoon or the letter to anyone. The letter was submitted by his younger brother, Dr Anthony McGuire of Prospect in Adelaide.

1916
SUNDAY, NOVEMBER 19
SOMEWHERE IN FRANCE

Dear Julian Thomas,

I have just received a letter from your God-Mother telling me of your entry into this world of (at present) strife and misery. And, my boy, I want to congratulate you on having such fine parents – and I want to say that you could not have chosen anyone better to mother you – and you have made me the proudest chap on this earth to know that you have chosen my name to carry you through the coming life of first innocence, happiness, trials. I hope with all my heart for as good an exit from this world as you have made an entry.

I am writing this well within reach of deadliest missiles you have not yet heard of. Snow is on the ground all around me. I'm seated in a miserable tent – on a cold muddy floor – and I can hardly hold this pencil in my fingers. Yet, my Jule, I feel that all this is absolute nothing compared with the pride I feel in having such a bonny boy as you are to look up to me and I make it my duty from this moment onwards to look on you as a special 'boy of mine'. And when you become old enough to know me – perhaps before even you see me, I want you to think of me as a great friend of yours and I want you to know that I will always have your welfare at heart.

Your mother and father have done me an honour I can't repay – by naming you after me after one so unworthy of that honour. But Julian, you and I are pals from this out and I know you will have a great good influence over me. Your first duty is to thank your mother and father for me – tell them in your own way – how proud I am of you and them. Then you must excuse the way this letter is written. But under the present circumstances it is impossible to do better. We are at present uncommonly close to our mutual enemy 'Fritz' and he is doing his best to kill as many of us as possible. But he won't get me. Though last night he dropped a huge shell within 50 yards of our dug out. He killed two and wounded 3 – made me duck. But I'm determined to see you Jule and so Fritz can go his hardest.

I'm so glad for your sake boy, that you have such fine Godparents. I'm afraid I'm a little jealous of you – but though you don't yet understand – I know you will love your God Mother as I can inform you she is unbeatable.

Your brothers, sisters and Joe, Dick, Dorothy, Molly, Alice and Marj – must be proud of you too! I know they will look after you – and you must ask them for me to send me a photo of yourself just as soon as is possibly convenient.

And now Jule, this is between the two of us – some day you will be able to read this letter for yourself – and if at that time both of us are still alive and well I want you to remind me of something I have on my mind to tell you! Your mother will keep this letter till then and one day she will let you read it. Then you must ask me.

I hope Julian my boy that long before you can talk openly – this beastly war, which is at present at its height, will be all settled and everyone peacefully settled down again. Then won't we two have some fine times together.

You will forgive me for not sending you some little present as yet and you will understand why when I tell you that there is nothing here hardly a tree standing, everything is sacked and torn by shot and shell. But Jule old chap – as soon as I get out of this inferno – somewhere near a civilised town – I will make it my business to send you some little token of my interest in you.

Give my love to Mother, Father, Dorothy, Joe, Molly, Dick, Alice, Marj and don't forget an extra large amount to your Godmother, and for yourself, Julian, heaps of my best love – and please permit me for all time to remain

Your very very best friend
Julian E. McGuire

Describing the brave death of a friend to console relatives back home was a grim task for many of our young soldiers during World War I. Here, JAMES SMITH, *of Toodyay, Western Australia, tells Annie Hassel (pictured), the mother of his 19-year-old mate Percy, why she should be proud of her eldest son. In doing so, he reveals in himself an awesome amount of stoicism and maturity. The holder of this letter, Patricia Lilleyman of Wembley in Perth, has not been able to trace whether James himself survived the war.*

1918
FEBRUARY 4
SOMEWHERE IN FRANCE

My dear Mrs Hassel,

You must think me a hard-hearted chap for not writing to you before and telling you how poor old Percy was killed. But the fact is we have been that busy in and out of the line up to now that I had hardly any chance of finding out. I received your letter today, so I am answering it straight away. Well, for the 20th of September our battalion had advanced closer on a mile. We took our objective alright with very slight casualties. Percy was alright up to then. Then the Germans organised a counter-attack and during the bombardment before they attacked (which was subsequently beaten back) Percy was killed. He was killed with a piece of a shell which burst not far from him. When night came on the boys went out and gave him a decent burial, which I am pleased to tell you. I was talking to an officer in his platoon (who has since been killed) just after we came out of the line on that occasion, and I was asking him about Percy. He told me that Percy was one of the best men in his platoon, also one of the bravest. So my dear Mrs Hassel you have something to be proud of in having a son like Percy. I know it must be hard for the dear mothers to lose

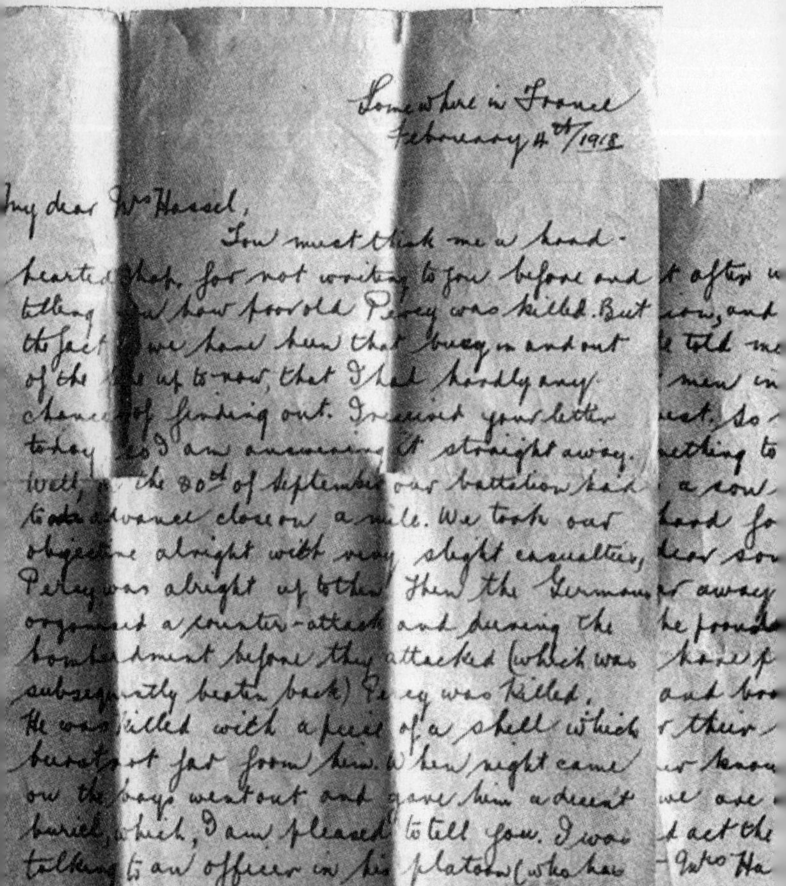

Somewhere in France
February 4th/1918

My dear Mrs Hassel,

You must think me a hard-hearted chap for not writing to you before and telling you how poor old Percy was killed. But the fact is we have been that busy in and out of the line up to now, that I had hardly any chance of finding out. I received your letter today so I am answering it straight away. Well, on the 30th of September our battalion had to advance close on a mile. We took our objective alright with very slight casualties, Percy was alright up to then. Then the Germans organised a counter-attack and during the bombardment before they attacked (which was subsequently beaten back) Percy was killed. He was killed with a piece of a shell which burst not far from him. When night came on the boys went out and gave him a decent burial, which, I am pleased to tell you. I was talking to an officer in his platoon (who has

sympathy

From
Yours ever Sincerely
A James Smith

their dear sons in this terrible war, and so far away from home. But they also should be proud of the fact that their sons, our sons, have played the game and died the best and bravest of deaths; that is, fighting for their loved ones and country. We never know when our turn may come. But we are all prepared to play the games and act the man right up to the last. Well, dear Mrs Hassel, I must close asking you to accept my deepest sympathy.

From Yours Ever Sincerely
A. James Smith

WILLIAM SIMMS *(pictured), the eldest of three children, wrote this letter to his widowed mother, Fanny Simms, from Germany, shortly after the end of World War I. It was written on the back of postcards of Cologne, Germany. Simms had served in France, Belgium and Germany, rising to the rank of lieutenant and being awarded a Distinguished Conduct Medal. He was wounded by shrapnel at Vimereux and had spent time in the UK recovering. While in England he joined the Infantry Cadet Battalion and was sent back to Belgium and Germany for the transition to peace. He arrived home in Melbourne in September 1919. This letter was contributed by William's granddaughter, Jane Wesson of Carine in Western Australia.*

7.5.1919
ZWEI-CAMPE HOTEL
COLOGNE
GERMANY

My Dear Mother

I've just written that address to more fully believe where I am. It's all all too strange beyond the most unbiassed expectations.

Reading ever so thoroughly the Peace Terms in the other day's paper amongst a rejoicing mixed population of Belgian English Colonial Yanks & French I had been forced to imagine directly opposite scenes in Germany. Yet now Ma I find my self in a beautiful country where everywhere is clean & bright & most everybody happy.

You'll find no traces of the war at all amongst the people nor even a shadow of worry or anxiety over the Peace Terms. In Belgium we had imagined with our neighbours – who hate them like poison – that they'd either all have long miserable faces or sing blood thirsty songs of hate & pray for a most awful anarchist revolution amongst their victors.

I suppose it's because our papers preached us a low decadent brutal enemy during the war that our enlightenment here was fraught with such tremendous spasms of surprise. Cos really we should not have been surprised every thing being of quite a simple & most human grade.

There was no need why Bosche gentlemen shouldn't have been courteous to women in the tram, train, public building & street or why the younger generation shouldn't be thoughtful & watchful for the old. Yet each instance gave us much food for reflection & consequential until later on our old & deep prejudices faded away & we felt in the midst of human beings equal to ourselves.

We were rather tickled by the amount of saluting forced upon us Ma, in fact our first day was so severe, we arranged that saluting in the future must be done in reliefs, and so we did & even then became awfully tired. Uniform is supplied to nearly all men who work out of doors in Germany & 'twas not only the quantity – cos there's policemen, railway officials, tram men, window cleaners, light lampers, street cleaners, newspaper vendors etc, but the quality that so amazed us. After continually hearing tales of a cloth famine being substituted by a paper variety we certainly didn't expect to find all these individuals wearing a nice spruce blue sort of woollen serge, with neat caps & brass buttons clean & bright.

Well to continue Ma, it's an order of the British Governor here that all Bosche in uniform must salute British officers – of which your son is a specimen, tho I'm afraid you doubt it Ma, judging by your determination to address letters to him as Cpl so & so. Well starting out from the station, we struck hordes of these 'blue birds' all religiously saluting us & looking quite respectful as they'd receive our dignified return. There's no need to say how [high] & mighty we felt with all this, and you can just imagine the shade of swagger it weaved into our step. This same step which we positively detest in foreigners, & most especially have we ridiculed & cheapened the Hun whenever he'd resorted to it.

But as I was saying, we felt 'some dogs' fully realizing our unique position & were contemplating upon our form of action should some disrespectful Hun fail in his duty. Oh we were going to be so awfully drastic & military 'we'd make an example etc' & 'show 'em what was what'.

But it was so much piffle & the wind blew it a way as such, cos I suppose it [shows] you fully well how obedient were the people it breathed upon & how ignorant were its visitors who couldn't even think reasonably. And to complete 'Saluting'. Tommy guards are all over the town, eyes ever watchful for Mr Samuel Brown to whom they click their heels & smack their rifles with quite an impressive & praiseworthy effect.

Of course while all these points attracted our attention we didn't fail to notice other things that make this city so beautiful. As usual with me cathedrals rank first & here we found one worthy of all attention, an object of great beauty as you'll see by the post cards. You could easily write a book on each day's events and impressions, so accept this brief glimpse now and I'll endeavour to take you all thro my journey – mentally – when I'm home.

Your loving son,
William

DAVID WESTGARTH *was still living at home with his parents in Scone, NSW, when his father, George (pictured), composed this letter to him, a page and a half of written words managing to convey more emotion between father and son than they would normally express in their daily conversations. David, who now lives in Bathurst, NSW, served in the Middle East as an aircraft gunner during the war, and later worked as a stock and station agent. At 79, he is still reluctant to talk about his wartime experiences. This letter was submitted by David's son, Stephen Westgarth, of Marrickville, Sydney.*

1941
DECEMBER 5
SCONE, NSW

My dear David,

This is to wish you a happy birthday and many happy returns. I enclose a copy of my father's Coat of Arms on which is the motto 'Mens Conscia Recti' meaning as you know 'A mind conscious of right'. Live up to it my son. I also give you my father's gold mounted crest which I hope you will appreciate as a family keepsake. The crest is engraved on a blood stone.

I shall now consent to your enlistment in the RAAF which you have wanted me to do for the last twelve months. I think 19 years old is young enough and I have given you time to think it over. You have your mother's pluck and my self-will and we are both very proud of you. Good luck and may God keep you safe my son. It will be the hardest thing that I have ever done when I sign the consent to your application.

Ever Your loving Dad
G.M. Westgarth

LIEUTENANT JOHN TRELEAVEN *wrote this letter to his eldest son, Nicholas, while stationed in Milne Bay, New Guinea, with the Australian Army Service Corps during World War II. Lieutenant Treleaven, who had enlisted in 1941, wrote regular letters home to his two boys, often decorating them with little drawings and once sending them a coconut, cherished to this day, with the postal address burnt into the side. He only met his second son, Peter, after being granted leave from Naval Base, just south of Fremantle, in 1942. John, 90 this year, and his wife, Margaret, 88, still live in the family home in Dianella, Perth. Nick, now 62, of North Beach, Perth, found this letter in an old folder of his school reports that his father gave him several years ago. His son, Edward, twelve, picked it up and read it out to him.*

WX 33594
2. Aust. Bulk Petroleum Storage Coy
AIF Australia
Milne Bay
25-10.43

My Dear Nicky,

Well my boy, on Monday the 1st Nov, you will be four years old. Gee son I do wish I could be home for your birthday, and that I could give you a present myself.

I daresay Mummy has something for you my boy, and your Daddy will bring you something home when he comes, but I am afraid you will have to wait quite a little time son, but never mind, for all good things are worth waiting for, believe me.

You see son there are no shops where your Daddy is stationed, so you see it is not possible to buy you anything, but you will understand I am sure, and be a good boy for Daddy.

Daddy is often wondering how you are, and what sort of new games you play. I bet you find young Peter a great playmate son, he will be able to help you with the little jobs you do for your mummy very soon now, won't he son.

Mummy is very lucky, for, to have two sons like you and Peter growing up, just think of all the pleasure you can give her, by that I mean, you must never forget, no matter how old you are, to always love her, and look after her, just as your Daddy would if he were home, for that is the main task your Daddy set for you my boy, and I know you will carry it out – I remember, or at least I think I do, when I was four years old, I had a birthday cake, made with three different coloured cakes. Rainbow cake they called it. It had four candles on it too. Gosh it

was fun trying to blow them all out at once too.

Hope you received the drawing I did for you in the last letter I wrote, I think you would like them son.

It will be nice living in Sth Perth, for mummy will be able to take you down swimming, but never go away without your Mummy will you son.

Well my boy, I guess I had better close, hope you have a nice birthday. Kiss Mummy and Peter and Grandma, and Grandpa for me son, the little birdies have told me you are being such a good boy so keep it up son, and all will be well.

God bless you, and Peter, and Mummy and keep you all safe till Daddy comes home again.

Lots of love
Daddy

LIEUTENANT KEITH MADIN *of the 4th Anti-Tank Regiment of the AIF wrote this touching letter to his wife Vera about rediscovering the simple things of life shortly after his release from the Kuching POW camp in Sarawak. After his return to Melbourne he completed his Bachelor of Arts degree, then studied theology as a curate and became an Anglican priest. He and Vera went on to have eight children (they are pictured overleaf with their daughter Alison). Tragically Keith died at the age of 42 of a brain haemorrhage, robbing Vera of much of that longed-for future together. They never went on a sea voyage. After Keith's death Vera, who now lives in Grovedale, Victoria, made use of her pharmacist qualifications and worked to support her children. This letter was contributed by the couple's daughter, Professor Alison Mackinnon of Glen Osmond, Adelaide.*

Monday 17.9.45
1830 hours

Vera

I'm beginning to know life again for I've just had a cold meat collation with many cups of tea and slices of bread and jam and now I'm sitting at a table in the lounge with a cigarette in my left hand as I write this the radio giving out the Andrews Sisters. I'm feeling a zest in things. Some events of today were breathtaking in the enjoyment I had from them – an issue of milk arrowroot biscuits, a cake of Nestle's Vitality chocolate, a long glass of beer (what smacking of lips went on after we quaffed that with rare abandon) and lying out on deck in an easy chair clad wholly in whites, the breeze just cool enough under the awnings, and watching islands slip by starboard and a great convoy heading in the opposite direction on the port side. Darling! That you were only with me! For what sea travel I've done gives me an appetite for more, and with you we shall see it!!

Sleep – the greatest curative of all. The clean white pyjamas on clean white sheets a soft white pillow with my cigarettes and matches beside me for that smoke during the night. The slipper question I've not got settled yet because I got very used to the wearing of native wooden clogs and as yet I've not got any slip-slops or chaplis – in any case things are so clean that yours truly hasn't worried and I enjoy padding around with my feet bare and unencumbered. This sort of letter writing can go on ad infinitum – do you mind? Bing Crosby has just given us something good – the boys observe that he is wearing well – I only know that I'm drinking it all in hungrily. I've seen some articles in the papers about the returned P.W. and how to treat him and put up with his strange whims and fancies – you won't be thinking of me as some strange creature will you Veest? For Alison to play with if he is tame enough?

One good thing has emerged though and that is that I'm a touch more modest being – not before time either – and there is much in my life that I'm going to construct and reconstruct in the course of the next few years, and I shall only be able to do it with your help, my darling wife.

The pay 'wallah' tells me I'm in possession of a fair bit of cash and with my allotments home (hinting at a saving wife) he led me to believe that I should do well from the Gov! However that's for the future – then we shall sit down and with lights turned low tot up our riches and have a real gloat as we used to in the old days of the flat in St Kilda. I'm an incurable romanticist darling: if not looking back looking forward and there's such a richness, plain and evident to me in our life together that I can look either way and draw comfort and love.

I can hardly believe all this at times – where is the barbed wire, the rice ration, the native gardening tools, the dirty clothes, the continual tension, the guards on their rounds? Which is the dream? So long have we sat by the waters of Babylon and wept that it is hard to believe that the Lord hath put his enemies to flight and lifted up the hearts of his chosen.

I have learned to know my God, darling wife, and my Lord Jesus is very close to me. In the communion of His love I pray for you always.

Keith

FRED McLELLAND *(pictured overleaf centre) wrote this letter from a prison camp in Thailand at the close of World War II. He and his childhood mate Norm Rafferty (on left) had been captured by the Japanese at the fall of Singapore in 1942 and interred in the Changi prison camp. They volunteered to work on the infamous Burma Railway after promises of more food and better conditions. Norm died on the railway; Fred dug his grave with his bare hands and buried him. Miraculously, Fred was able to keep a letter that Norm had written to his mother throughout the years of his internment. He delivered this letter on his return home and it remains in the possession of Norm's family today. Fred, who was known as Ev to his family and Mac to his mates, survived and went on to marry and have two children. He died in November 2000 at the age of 82. His daughters, Robyn Higgins of Alice Springs and Janis Jackson of Springwood, NSW, contributed this letter.*

1945
SEPTEMBER 4
THAILAND

Dear Mum, Dad and Joyce

Well thank goodness that's over. How are you all – it is some time since I had any of your letters, all of which were about one year old – in all I have received about ten letters from you. This does not look many but there are a large number of the boys who have not had any – our hosts, the yellow, did not agree with mail.

When the war ended I was in a working camp in the jungle, we were making a drome. On the 16th of August we lined up for work and after waiting over an hour were broken off and told later we would receive good news. Two hours later we were told there would be no more work. It was not for about five days that the Nips told us that the war was officially over. However after the first day we knew that the yellow fiend was finished. Since then I have moved to a base camp where conditions are improved. We are still living on the products of the land but as we are receiving all the rations we want are eating well. Planes have dropped medical gear and a very small quantity of tinned food. The latter we drew for and I received a tin of stew and my mate a packet of biscuits so we've done OK.

We have a wireless in the camp now – and so news is issued three times a day – the only thing we want to know is when we are going home. Some have left for India, some Rangoon but the order came that all Australians were to wait for orders from Australia so now we are just waiting longing for news from you. I have so many questions to ask when I see you.

How is Les, send my love and tell her I will write as soon as possible, we are only allowed one letter just now. I suppose Diana and Allan are both big kids now.

When I arrive home Dad you will have to take some long leave so we can all have a holiday to remember. On reading this letter it seems poor but forgive me this time, it is hard to get the mind to work, everywhere the boys are writing and asking each other how to spell this and that.

Don't worry over me I am 100% fit and only longing for the day when I can get my arms around you all.

All the love in the world, Ev

P.S. I will also get in touch with the Raffertys as soon as possible. Norm died at Tavoy – Burma on 4/10/42. He was a real mate and I missed him for some time.

PETER LAST *of Unley Park in Adelaide wrote this letter to his eleven-year-old son Robert in July 1967, soon after arriving with the Australian Surgical Aid Team at a civilian hospital in Bien Hoa, 25 kilometres from Saigon, during the Vietnam War. There were three large American 'evac' hospitals nearby, from which there was always a spillover of civilian and military casualties, brought in by the Medivac choppers from war zones. The children's ward was an old rice store with an unlined roof and floored with badly laid bricks. There were 30 cots, with an average occupancy of about 45 patients, as well as family members, who provided primary care for the patients. When Peter (pictured with another member of the Surgical Aid Team), a father of four, returned to his job as Senior Specialist Physician at Repatriation General Hospital Daw Park, and Honorary Physician to Royal Adelaide Hospital, he tells of having experienced significant 're-entry' problems, having grown accustomed to diagnosing patients without any equipment or lab results. In 1991, Peter was awarded an OAM for his services to medicine.*

BIEN HOA
SOUTH VIETNAM
6 July 1967

My Dear Rob,

This letter should reach you about the time of your [eleventh] birthday, and I do hope that it is a happy one for you. Although I am so far away, living a strange, exciting and very different life, I think all the time about home and I wonder how you all are. I have my two pictures of [my yacht] Kareelah on the wall, and beside me as I write are photographs of you all that I took last year while we were caravanning in the Flinders. You may remember one of them taken on a peak overlooking Parachilna Gorge, when we could see for miles and there was nobody else anywhere in sight. It would be hard for you to imagine a greater contrast to this country, where you can never get away from crowds and crowds of people, and where life is in every way so different.

As I write, I can hear the regular firing of nearby howitzers, sending shells out into the night, mostly firing at one of the rivers nearby, down which the Viet Cong bring their supplies at night. I have learned to tell the different thump of a mortar bomb, which may be ours or theirs, and occasionally there is the rattle of machine gun fire, usually from the river half a mile away. It has been raining very heavily for four hours, and the power failed until a few minutes ago, probably because one of the poles had been hit by lightning. Because of the rain, this is the first night that there hasn't been a steady flutter of helicopters – usually the little three or four-seaters, but occasionally the big Chinooks, which can take a whole tank or a truck load of troops and all their gear. Fighter jets (F100s) and bombers, enormous transport planes (like pregnant whales with wings) and little scouting high-winged monoplanes pass over all the time, and the air traffic is as heavy as the buses down King William Street at rush hour. Vietnamese and American soldiers are everywhere, often armed with rifles, pistols or machine guns, and I often see jeeps with a radio aerial and a machine gun, just like your model.

In a way this is very exciting, and from TV shows like 'Combat' you might think that war is a dashing and heroic sort of business. I haven't seen any fighting, of course, and I hope very much that I won't have to, but daily I see the results. It is all very well for the heroic actor, but for the person hit it is just painful and horrible. I would like you to meet Gna Van Nguyen, who is about your age. He was playing with a grenade, probably playing soldiers, just as you do. But this one went off. It blew out an eye, part of his skull, several fingers, and left bits of metal in his arms, legs and belly muscles. Yesterday I saw a girl a bit younger, who almost had her leg cut off by a hatchet after her mother had been murdered, and a lad of about ten who drove his motorcycle under a truck and had both legs broken.

I know that you are old enough to understand that you are fantastically lucky. You have a whole large room to yourself. Your only real danger comes from riding your bicycle to school or falling off the roof. Here a whole family may live in a space smaller than your room, and they live every day with violence and death. We can take you off cruising in Kareelah or to the James family on their farm, where you have space, security and freedom. Here there are no holidays, and never any chance – and probably no desire – to be relatively alone in the world. Yet these people are happy and very brave, for they live always with suffering, death and alien people about them. My crowded, dirty and hot children's ward is happy, and I have yet to hear a child grizzle or nag its parents or elder brothers and sisters who actually care for it.

Imagine that Billy [aged four] broke his leg and went to hospital. You would stay home from school to sit on or beside his bed all day. Most of the time you would be fanning him to relieve the heat, except when you were fetching and emptying his pot, preparing his food or cleaning his dishes. Each afternoon and perhaps overnight you would crowd in with him to sleep in your clothes on a rubber mattress with no sheets in a cot less than five feet long and designed to take only one child. When he left hospital, you might carry him home on your back, or you might be lucky enough to take him on your motorcycle, for many boys of your age ride them about the streets of the city and on the roads to Saigon.

In addition to this, some friend or relative might be shot or stabbed, mutilated, perhaps killed. I would be away, as my new friend, Dr Tuan has been, for ten years of military service in the Air Force – almost your whole life. Mum would be left alone with the family, as I have done for this brief three months.

So naturally I wonder what sort of world you will grow up in, and whether you or your children may ever face anything like what has happened to these brave and happy people. I want you to know that there are people all over the world with some sort of problems such as those here, although very few as bad – in Africa, the Middle East and South America. I want you to know that you are lucky to be so wonderfully privileged. I want you to be as happy as you can, trying to remember the good times and the people you like best. Particularly I want you to know what it is to have a family about you, and to be happy with your sisters and brother – not squabbling over little things that don't matter, and always remembering that we are a family, that we should help, support and love each other, and make it our job to stick together.

I am sure that while I am away I can rely on you to help Mum, to take my place at the head of the table, and to take the responsibility of being the head of the family. Please be very careful riding your bicycle to school, although your traffic could not compare with this, where small vehicles give way to big, and children and animals don't give way to anything.

I have written you this long and serious letter because I want you to start to think of the wide world outside family and school and Adelaide. Naturally I am very careful in the way I live here and I take no risks, but war is a dangerous business, even for civilians like us. I know that I may get hurt or even killed. So I want you to know my feelings on these serious subjects, in case it may be hard for me to explain them later.

Please look after Mum, Katherine, Anne, Bill and Angus [the dog] and the rabbit. Have a happy birthday, and write to tell me all the things that have been happening.

Love from Dad

JOHN QUILTY *(pictured in uniform in Vietnam) was in the very first call-up to national service in response to the Vietnam War. The year was 1965 and John was just twenty. As he was studying an agricultural science degree at university at the time, he was granted a deferment. Two years later, degree under his belt, John entered the army and the following year saw a seven-month tour of duty in Vietnam. During this posting he wrote many lively letters home to his parents, including this one from Saigon. Although John, who runs his own environmental consultancy, grew up in Lindfield, Sydney, he and his wife, Lyn, whom he married in 1975, moved to the Perth suburb of Warnbro in 1978. The couple have seven children, ranging in age from 13 to 29, and three grandchildren aged 1 to 4.*

SAIGON – 1968
HQAFV
AFPO1
Monday 5 Aug

Dear Mum, Dad & Boys,

Been quiet up here most of the week and an air of expectancy over the place at the moment as the 3rd offensive is awaited, though exactly when it will start, if at all, is subject to conjecture. Odd rumours add fuel to the fire, but surprisingly enough such rumours aren't rife on the whole.

Had the day off today and went out to Saigon Zoo this morning. Not exactly crowded with animals, but a reasonable selection and well laid out, with spreading lawns and gardens, not the tar and cement which typifies Taronga. Even a 'roo in one compound, a more dejected 'roo I've never seen. Seems criminal to sentence an animal from the open spaces of Australia to this place, but then guess the same could be said for any animal in any zoo. Conducted around the zoo by a bunch of scruffy children who assaulted in force with bags of peanuts to offer the moment I set foot inside the gate.

Some of these children on the streets, particularly the younger ones around 5 & 6, are almost impossible to turn away. With their big, innocent pleading eyes, they have a great psychological advantage over their adult counterparts, and, unlike some of the older folk, are always friendly and never bear any malice towards the foreign troops. Like children the world over, though a good deal broader perhaps in outlook and 'education' (for want of a better term). Many could virtually fend for themselves from the day they start to walk – give perhaps a year or two.

Met up with a Yank there with no racial prejudice, and no desire to spout off about the 'bigness' of the States (despite the fact that he was from Texas which one Yank told us takes 6 days to cross – on foot no doubt!) Very refreshing to yarn to, and we had a feed in Saigon then went on to the USO Club.

Actually find most Yanks here very friendly, and provided they're not led on they won't usually start spouting about the Mother country. When they do start, some of our mob can be just as bad spouting back about Australia. Have met one or two with racial prejudices who were a trial to tolerance to listen to, but here again such individuals with extreme views aren't struck too often. I think quite a few, like this bloke I met today, probably modify their opinions when they join the Army and are obliged to work and fight alongside Negroes.

Sending some photos and slides which may be of interest. Most of them were taken in and around Saigon. Photos should arrive about the same time as this, but slides may be a bit slower in coming.

Love
John

Letters from Family

WILLIAM JOHN WILLS *wrote this letter to his father Dr William Wills shortly before dying of starvation at Cooper Creek, South Australia, in 1861. He and fellow explorer Robert O'Hara Burke had just led the first crossing of the continent south to north, enduring the worst kind of privations in their quest. Against all the odds they managed to survive the return journey south to their base camp at Cooper Creek, only to discover their support party had left a few hours earlier; the coals were still warm in the fire. The leader of the support party, William Brahe, who had been employed by the explorers over a beer in a pub, had grown sick of waiting and was worried he and his men were not going to be paid. Burke and Wills starved to death within weeks, refusing the help of local Aborigines. This letter is in the Australian Manuscripts Collection, State Library of Victoria (MS9504) and is printed with the permission of the Library Board of Victoria. Simon Longstaff's 1907 depiction of the doomed explorers is from the National Gallery of Victoria.*

27 JUNE 1861

My dear Father

These are probably the last lines you will ever get from me. We are on the point of starvation not so much from absolute want of food but from the want of nutriment in what we can get.

Our position although more provoking is probably not near so disagreeable as that of poor Harry & his companions; We have had every good luck and made a most successful trip to Carpentaria and back to where we had every right to consider ourselves safe. Having left a Depot here consisting of four men twelve horses and six camels, they had sufficient provisions to have lasted them for twelve months with proper economy. We had also every right to expect that we should have been immediately followed up from Mininda [Menindie] by another party with additional provisions and every thing necessary for forming a permanent Depot at Coopers Creek. The party we left here had special instructions not to leave until our return, unless from absolute necessity. We left the Creek with, nominally, three months supply, but they were reckoned at little over the rate of half rations & we calculated on having to eat some of the Camels. By the greatest good luck at every turn we crossed to the Gulf through a good deal of fine country almost in a straight line from here. On the other side the camels suffered considerably from wet & we had to kill & jerk one soon after starting back. We had now been out a little more than two months and found it necessary to reduce the rations considerably, and this began to tell on all hands, but I felt it by far less than either of the others. The great scarcity & shyness of game & our forced marches prevented our supplying the deficiency from external sources to any great extent but we never could have held out but for the Crows & Hawks & the Portulac. The latter is an excellent vegetable and I believe secured our return to this place. We got back here in four months & four days and found that the party had left the creek the same day & we were not in a fit state to follow them.

I find I must close this that it may be planted [buried] but I will write some more although it has not so good a chance of reaching you [then follow two words which are illegible in the pencil-written original].

You have great claim on the Committee for their neglect. I leave you the sole charge of what is coming to me the whole of my money I desire to leave to my sisters. Other matters I will leave for the present.

Adieu My Dearest Father
W.J. Wills

I think to live about four or five days. My religious views are not the least changed and I have not the least fear of their being so. My spirits are excellent.

JOHN DUNN, *1846–66, was the eldest son of convict parents. He joined Ben Hall's gang of bushrangers in 1864 and during his brief career was involved in many raids and robberies. In January 1865 he shot dead Constable Nelson of Collector, near Goulburn, NSW. He was captured the following December and sentenced to death. Dunn (of whom this sketch was made at the time for a newpaper) was executed on 19 March 1866. He was just nineteen. This letter was written while he was awaiting execution in Sydney's Darlinghurst Jail and reveals Dunn's sensitivity to his mother's grief. In it he warns his father that although he would be 'gratified' to see his mother before he dies he does not want her to witness his execution. The original letter is held in the Mitchell Library, State Library of New South Wales (ML MSS 5518).*

1866
2nd MARCH
GAOL, SYDNEY

My dear Father,

I received your very welcome second letter a few days ago – I say welcome although it conveyed to me the death of my sister. I can sincerely condole with you on this bereavement coming too at such a time, but you will remember that I never saw my little sister and therefore it is why I state that any letter from you under my circumstances is welcome.

I have not yet heard what day is fixed for my execution but it cannot be far off as I was told by Father Dwyer last evening that he had an interview with the Prime Minister and that the law is to take its course.

Under the circumstances it will be advisable for you to come down with my brother without delay – Mother knows how gratified I would be to see her before I die, but don't let her come. It is best not. I can bid goodbye to you for her, and send her a keepsake by you also. So reason with her about it and persuade her to remain at home. I have no more to say in this letter. As soon as I hear of 'the day' I will let you know.

With love to all
believe me dear father
your affectionate Son
John Dunn

ARCHIBALD HENRY McVICAR *was one of eleven surviving children of a poor Anglo-Scottish immigrant couple living on the former goldfields in the Victorian Pyrenees. His mother produced a child every second year between 1854 and 1881, mostly while teaching school at the remote village of Mountain Hut, now gone. The school records show she enrolled some of her children when they were two years of age. In 1878, at the age of fourteen, Archibald and his twenty-year-old brother, James, went to cut timber on the other side of the mountain range from Mountain Hut. Family lore has it that they communicated with the family via letters carried in a cylinder on the collar of a dog (Pedro) that knew to go between Mountain Hut and their current camp. It is thought that the 'flock' referred to was a flock of kangaroos. Arch grew up to have eight children of his own. At age 47, he moved to the Mallee to take up virgin ground for his family near what is now Underbool. There he farmed and participated in the development of the town, and continued to ride a horse until not long before his death in 1954, aged 90. His descendants still farm the original Mallee settler blocks. This letter was contributed by a grandson, Ian McVicar of Underbool.*

1878
SUNDAY 14TH

Dear Father and Mother,

Pedro came out on the Monday night. Will you go to Mr Scott's and get Jamsie's boots if they are finished and send them out as quick as possible for he is quite barefooted. And also send his best shirt and scarf and a piece of writing paper and an envelope. We will not be home till we finish here. If you could send a few shillings out to us it would be very convenient for it is a long way to come home and then come back again. When you are sending the boots and things, direct them to the Post Office Redbank, care of Mr Murphy.

We have a job to get meat now as our flock has decamped to another hill. I have no more to say at present so I must conclude sending our best love to you all I remain

Your affectionate son
Arch. McVicar

In 1897, MARIANN HUMBY, *accompanied by her eight-year-old daughter Josie, went to Sydney to give birth at a hospital in Darlinghurst. Here, Josie writes to her father Charles back in Indooroopilly, Queensland, about her mother remaining ill in hospital after the child is stillborn. The reference to burning papers is obscure, other than its being some form of child's amusement. Josie would return to Sydney twelve years later to marry Bernard Bede Tuohy and settle in the suburb of Mosman. She remained in Sydney until her death at the age of 80 in 1969. The letter was submitted by Diana Rother, Josie's granddaughter, of Buderim, Queensland.*

1897
SEPTEMBER 12

My dear Papa,

You know about poor mama being in the hospital, and she is very bad yet, Auntie and I spend two hours with her every day. We think she will soon be better now. I received the little music books you sent, also the table book, and the papers which I burnt next morning, I burnt three or four to see if they were all the same, and they were, the four were mens heads.

At night I went down stairs to show Mrs Pennington's little daughter how they burnt, I burnt two, the first one I burnt was a mans head. I am learning my lessons very well and I am getting on with my tables. We feel very miserable here without mama. I cannot write you a long letter this time dear papa as it is nearly my bed time so I must close with lots of love and xxxxxxxx

I remain your loving daughter, Josie

EMILY HARTLEY, *of Enfield in Sydney, writes to her daughter Teresa Magnussen in Broken Hill wishing her well during a forthcoming childbirth. She needn't have worried. The baby, Consett Hartley Magnussen, the second of her three children, survived, and lived to the age of 71. He is pictured here with his mother and younger brother Walter. This letter was submitted by Trish Magnussen of Bonython in Canberra, the wife of Consett's son, Robin Magnussen.*

1899
AUGUST 30
ENFIELD, SYDNEY

My dear Daughter,

I have been waiting to hear the news. I hope by this time your dear little Baby has arrived safely, and that you my dear are doing well, and are happy. It is wearying waiting the last week or two, (but everything comes to them that wait).

I am glad you have such nice things for it, you are like myself I love a Baby to look nice, I hope you will soon get strong again, you will have nice cool weather that is one comfort, I hope dear old Bas, will soon be better I am sure he worries alot about you being ill, I know it is hard for both of you not having a little mine money I wish I could help you, I may some day. Mon dear I must tell you about myself, I am a deal better, the medicine is doing me such a lot of good. I am able to walk without much pain and I begin to eat and sleep better, I am to keep on taking the same stuff for twelve months to get it out of my system but I won't mind that as long as I am able to do my work and go to Church, the Garden is beginning to look lovely I hope some day soon, you will be able to see it and then I may see baby.

Charlie and Artie send their love to you both.

Hoping to hear good news from you, may God bless you is the prayer of your loving Mother.

Emily Hartley

ALICE HARRIET BRICE *(pictured) wrote this letter to her daughter-in-law Violet Georgia in June or July of 1926. Violet was married to Alice's son Clem and the couple were expecting their first child. Alice, who taught herself to read and write as her six children were growing up, was delighted that her son and his wife were so happy as Clem had been in his thirties and a confirmed bachelor before meeting Violet. The pretty seventeen-year-old had caught his eye as she served in the Army and Navy Store in Berri on the Murray in South Australia. Family legend has it that the moment he laid eyes on her he declared: 'That is the girl I am going to marry.' And despite the difference in their ages, he did. They went on to have three children. This letter was contributed by Evelyn Campbell, the baby for whom the cap and coat were intended, who is now 75, has four grown-up sons and lives in Warradale, Adelaide.*

1926
ADELAIDE

My dear Vi,

This is just a little cap to ware with the little coat I sent you. Clem has gone in to have his teeth seen to, my word he is looking fat and well. I do not know what you give him to eat but what ever it is he looks wonderfuly well. He says you give him rubarb some times and it is very nice. Well he has been singing your prases all the time he has been home and I feel very happy to know you and my son are so happy in your nice little home. My very best love to you dear, Clem will tell you all the news.

Ever your loving
Mater

OFFLAND DUTTON *wrote this letter to his niece Clara Lavercombe (pictured) in 1941. In it he urges Clara, who was 38 at the time, to marry before she is too old and not to waste her life. Clara did not heed this advice. Neither she nor her two brothers, Hugh and Frank, married, but lived out their days in the family home at Mount Hunter in the Camden region of NSW. Their father, Edward, had been the town's blacksmith. Clara died in 2000, aged 91. This letter was found among her belongings and is held by The Oaks Historical Society at the Wollondilly Heritage Centre. Offland Dutton had recently sold his dairy farm at Coorabell in northern NSW and moved to Mullumbimby, just south of the NSW–Queensland border.*

Whian Street
MULLUMBIMBY
20.9.41

My Sweetest of Sweets,

I must apologise for not answering your last letter really, I forgot all about it, you can quite understand my position, when I was on the farm, I had the cows to attend to, pigs and calves, and green feed to grow and feed, and had a cream run to Mullumbimby as well, in fact I was going like a scalded cat every day and well into the night at times, so you must excuse me for being forgetful. Its not that I dont think of you, I do, and I think very often that its time you were getting married, you won't always have your parents to live with, and why waste your life while you are young, nobody wants any of us when we grow old, its what you might term the tradgery [tragedy] of life. So buck up darling and get a life partener and strike out for yourselves you will never do it younger and may you get someone that is worthy of you.

Well I sold out at Coorabell last November and I came down to Mullumbimby to live. I work on a banana plantation at Mullumbimby Creek, it's a good free life. I only work five days a week eight hours a day. The job is permanent for the duration of the war. I have a nice little sedan car Wyllies 77 I drive backwards and forwards every day to my work so I am at home all the week. Aunty Clara has a much better life in town. She has no cows to woory her. She keeps a few white leghorns and puts her time in the garden she has the water laid on and electricity so I guess she would not swap places with the dairy farm. Reg is building a house for himself on his fifty acre farm down at Byron Bay he hopes to complete it by the end of the month. I am enclosing a snap of Hope and Edna and one of Hope by her self and its the living picture of her, I got a letter from Dick Hamer a few days ago, I was very pleased to hear from him, they were very kind to me when I was down four years ago and I hope to repay them some day if ever I get the chance.

Well darling I must close trusting you are ok and remember me to all the family.

Yours affectionately, Offland

NORMAN JOHNSTONE *and* WILMA BECK *met in Adelaide in 1942, where Norm was stationed after being shipped back from the Middle East. Wilma's mother was a member of the Comforts Fund, which organised outings for soldiers staying in the city. The couple met when the Beck family hosted a tennis gathering at their home – Wilma was 19, Norm was 25. Soon after, Norman was sent to Darwin and the betrothed couple corresponded for a year before marrying in Adelaide in June 1943. They had only three weeks of married life before Norman was again shipped off, eventually to New Guinea. His father, George, penned this letter to Wilma after the announcement of their engagement in January 1943. Norman's four sisters also wrote congratulatory letters to Wilma on her engagement. George Johnstone, a magistrate, died in 1945 before Norman had returned from New Guinea. After the war, Norman and Wilma settled in Newport, Sydney, where they have lived for 53 years. They have four daughters and a son. Norman worked as a bank manager and after retirement went into the newsagency business.*

1943
JANUARY 30
CREMORNE, SYDNEY

My dear Wilma,

I am the father of your betrothed – NX6036, Johnstone, N.M. According to his last letter you have accepted his 117th proposal. So, my dear little girl, I want to congratulate you most sincerely upon your engagement and to express the hope that, until your next meeting, you will continue to carry on this furious love-making by post and that then Norm's wish for the marriage to take place during his next leave will come true. Then should that be the case, my next wish is the best thing the world has to offer – a happy married life.

I suppose dear old Norm has his faults but as a son and brother he is a most lovable chap and we are all very fond of him and he of us. Like his good little mother before him his ethics are of the highest and, although he was always a great fellow for dancing and mixing, he has always seemed to me to be very decidedly a one-woman man.

Last Sunday I was listening to the radio and a chap was talking about happiness. He quoted Robert Louis Stevenson as saying something to the effect that very few ever catch up with happiness, that not happiness itself but the pursuit of happiness was the really great thing, and that it was better to journey hopefully than to arrive. Norm seems to have had a great time in the pursuit of happiness since he met you. I hope that you have too. But I do hope also, with all my heart, that you both arrive.

Yours sincerely
George Johnstone

The year was 1969 and CAMBRIA PARKINSON, *a young wife and mother living on a farm near Kergunyah on the NSW–Victoria border, felt torn between the needs of her husband and children and the needs of her father, Frank Donovan, after the sudden death of her mother. Cambria had left Melbourne two years earlier, age twenty-four, and moved to the Wodonga area. Her husband Cliff had a job on a farm and the young family lived in an old wooden cottage in the Kiewa Valley. Frank, a veteran of World War I and approaching eighty, was living on his own for the first time. This letter was contributed by Cambria's sister, Annette Culley, of Heathmont in Victoria. Cambria and Cliff (pictured overleaf in their early married life), both approaching sixty, now live on the edge of the Brisbane Ranges National Park in Victoria. Since then they have named two of their dwellings Kergunyah.*

SAME PLACE
Friday, August 8
1969

Dearest Dad,

Just a couple of pages of news this time because I'm tired after shopping today and it is now after 9pm. How are you (all) getting on? I think of you every day, and wonder how you are.
We are well, although my sore throat is still hanging around (that sounds funny, doesn't it?). I know you cannot write very often, dear, but even a small note occasionally would do. I really don't mind writing 2 or 3 letters in a row.

The piano finally arrived safely after the driver, dithering around supposedly trying to find Kergunyah and ended up dumping it at the Albury depot at night time and disappeared off to Melb. again! He skited that he had loaded it on his own – all 2 tons of it!! They reckon he's a bit of a dill up here and we were very worried for a while. Anyhow, the fellows from Albury branch did a fantastic job delivering it and it was such a job and such a cold foggy old morning, I made a wood fire in the lounge, and they had a cup of tea. All told, they were here for over one hour! My little 'Gors and Kallman' piano has gone off to be sold – I only want $50 for it as it needed such a lot done to it and we paid only $90 for it in Boronia. My magnificent 'Beale' now stands proudly in the lounge and I have played it every day and am even getting my old touch back again. Perhaps I can make mummy happy now, by trying to play to a better standard. She always told me how disappointed she was with my playing.

I shall treasure it till I die and perhaps can pass it on to my daughter, who knows?

Christopher is growing more adorable every day, and is full of cheek and smiles. He seems to know my face and looks really pleased to see me when I come to look at him. I took him to CWA yesterday and everyone was nursing him and talking to him. One person even commented on how bright he is!

Football finishes tomorrow with a barbecue here tomorrow night. I am relieved, as now Cliff can get a little bit done around the place. The windows are nearly all repaired and I am making white curtains trimmed in black and white check gingham, for the back verandah. It will then look like a real sunroom or breakfast room. It's really lovely and sunny in the mornings. Cliff wants to put in a strip heater so we can move the kitchen table back out there. It's great fun doing all these things to the place – even though it isn't our house.

Well, spring is almost here, with the lawn dreadfully long already, and all the weeping willows in bud. It really gives my spirit a lift, as the winter here is so cold and miserable. The forecast tonight is for snow in N.E. so I think nature may be a bit early! Two swallows have been busy building under our outside verandah and making a dreadful mess. They also sleep tucked up high in the rafters.

I haven't had any letters at all this week, but received about 10 cards of sympathy. I am still living in a state of shock, I am sure, and almost go crazy thinking of mummy all day as I am working. I just can't imagine it's all happened that I'll never see her handwriting on a letter again, never see her smiling face at your door again. I do hope this sadness passes, but as one lady friend said 'you'll think of her every day of your life – you've just got to accept it'. Kathleen and I picked a lovely bunch of purple violets the other day and K. said 'for Grandma' after I suggested it. I hated throwing them out.

Well, darling, I know Annette is looking after everything well, poor pet, she seems to be doing so much and I nothing. I hope it will be much easier for her when they move in.

I must close now, dad, and I hope you and everyone are well. Give my love to them,

Yours lovingly,
Cambria. xxxx

There was barely a dry eye in the house when Nicholas Reid opened a present from his grandmother at his twenty-first birthday in Sydney in 1996. MARGARET MANEA *had died four years earlier, aged 67, and this letter from her dropped out of the copy of* The Sydney Morning Herald *she had saved for him the day he was born. Nicholas was Margaret's first-born grandchild, the son of Anne and Ron Reid. He now works in advertising in Sydney.*

1975
FEBRUARY 28

My Darling Grandson,

I wrapped this *Herald* up the day you were born, to be presented to you on your 21st birthday. I thought you would be interested in the headlines on the day you were born. At this stage I haven't seen you yet, your Father just rang me to say you had arrived in the world.

What a day it has been, I haven't left the phone all day, waiting for news of you. Your Mother hasn't been out of my thoughts all day. It is pouring rain, it hasn't stopped all day. I can't tell you what I felt when I got the news of your arrival. All I can say, is I love you very much. I hope you give your mother the love and happiness that she has given to me over the years. You see I love her very much. I hope you travel a straight, healthy road along life's way.
Well my grandson, all My Love.

Your ever loving
Grandmother

AUSTRALIAN
PRODUCTS
ARE
EXCELLENT

Letters from Home

In 1973 Patrick White was awarded the Nobel Prize for Literature. The chaos that followed is described by White in this letter to Tom Maschler, who was the chairman of Jonathan Cape publishers, which accepted The Vivisector, *the first of the White novels it published.*

We follow with a letter White wrote in 1918 as a six-year-old to Father Xmas. He was a gifted wordsmith even at that tender age. Patrick White died in 1990. Permission to publish granted by Barbara Mobbs of Paddington, Sydney, and the State Library of NSW (ML MSS 5719).

Centennial Park
Sydney
23.10.1973

Dear Tom,

I was glad to get your reactions to The Cockatoos. I had begun to grow very despondent as the result of the typescript's taking six weeks to arrive, then the postal strike here, closing of the airport during the radar technicians strike, in fact every possible obstacle to receiving news of anything from anyone. At one stage it took letters six days to cross the Harbour.

Thank you for your telegram on my receiving IT. I spent a very strenuous and alarming Thursday night and all day Friday. The press began pounding on the door about 9pm and Manoly [White's partner] found out what it was about. I had gone to bed with a sleeping pill after cleaning the house all day and wasn't going to come down for anybody. They rampaged round the house, ringing bells, pounding doors, and making the dogs bark for at least an hour and a half. Once when I looked out there were about twenty people camped on the lawn, and others on the terrace at the back. I almost didn't dare grope my way downstairs in the dark to get at the whisky. Next morning at six o'clock they started coming back, and during the day I received six television teams, three radio interviewers, all the local newspapers, Newsweek, and a lady from Finland. Now things are calmer, but I have a drawerful of letters and telegrams to deal with, and am expected to judge a play competition, address political demonstrations, and hand over the prize-money to nuns who appear on my doorstep. (I have a plan for using the prize-money which is now being discussed with one or two people I am asking to help.)

Well, that is that. I am amazed at the way Australians have reacted, in a way they usually behave only for swimmers and athletes. I am very touched, and have been feeling guilty for some of the things I have said about them in the past. On Sunday Manoly and I went to a concert given by the Moscow Chamber Orchestra and people kept coming up wanting me to sign their programmes. One of my journalist friends says I am the only person ever to have upstaged the Queen.

Shall be glad when the 4th November is here and we leave for a couple of weeks in Tasmania.

Yours, Patrick.

Yes, this war [the Yom Kippur War] — I am torn between wanting it to stop and hoping to see the Israelis into Cairo and Damascus before that happens.

1918
DECEMBER

Dear Father Xmas,
  Will you please bring me
  a pistol, a mouth organ
  a violin
  a butterfly net
  Robinson Cruso
  History of Australia
  Some marbles
  a little mouse that run across the room
  I hope you do not think I am too greedy but
I want the things badly

  Your loving
  Paddy

Childhood has not changed much in a century and a half. Here MARION COX *lovingly tells her mamma what occupied the mind of a nine-year-old in 1851. This letter and photograph of Marion are held by the Archives Office of Tasmania (NS1640/72).*

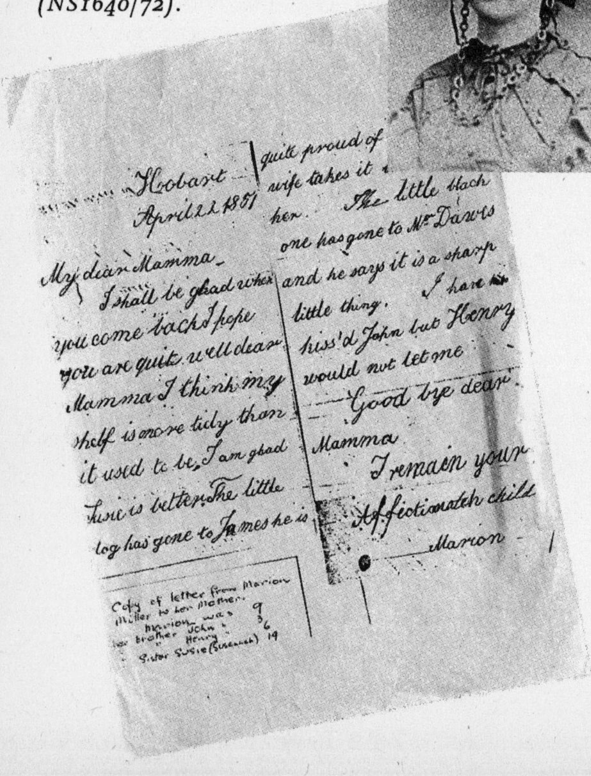

Hobart
April 22 1851

My dear Mamma
I shall be glad when you come back I hope you are quite well dear Mamma I think my shelf is more tidy than it used to be, I am glad Susie is better The little dog has gone to James he is quite proud of ... wife takes it ... her. The little black one has gone to Mr Davis and he says it is a sharp little thing. I have kiss'd John but Henry would not let me
Good bye dear Mamma
I remain your
Affectionate child
Marion

Copy of letter from Marion Miller to her mother.
Marion was 9
her brother John " 3
" Henry " 6
Sister Susie (Susannah) 14

1851
APRIL 22
HOBART

My Dear Mamma,

I shall be glad when you come back. I hope you are quite well dear Mamma. I think my shelf is more tidy than it used to be. I am glad Susie is better. The little dog has gone to James he is quite proud of it and his wife takes it to bed with her. The little black one has gone to Mr Daves and he says it is a sharp little thing. I have kiss'd John but Henry would not let me.

Good bye dear Mamma.
I remain your affectionate child, Marion

Unfortunately, little is known about the author of this letter, WILLIAM LORENZO COX *(on rocking horse surrounded by siblings). What we do know is that 'Willie' was ill at the time of writing and confined to his bed and that his mother was absent from the home.*

We also know, from his letter, that the remarkable candour of children has remained unchanged. The original letter and photograph are held by the Archives Office of Tasmania (NS164/72).

1922
MONDAY
LINDISFARNE, WESTON

Dear Mum,

I hope you are getting on all right and enjoying your holidays. I would like to be up there with you as long as I didn't have to go to school. As it happens I am not at school. I've got a sore throat and when I sneeze I get a headache. I am in your bed so you see I've got the ink here. Nellie and Girlie have gone up the hill and Georgie is chopping wood. It is about half past five and the sun has set. We got the photos of our house on Saturday and if you look hard down by the red gate you can see Betty Burrows. Nellie is getting on well with the housekeeping we have hot dinners every day and an apple pie or a pudding of some sort. Dad said you were going to get some postcards and send them down to us. If you send me one I hope it is a photo of some place. Nellie told me not to write you a letter because she said that you said you were going to forget us but I am writing one all the same. Dicky thinks he is boss now you are away, he says that we must do as he says. Freddie was kind enough to give me an anaceed just when I didn't want it and other times he wouldn't if I asked him. Wattle is out down here and Basil is sticking it in his socks etc. I think this is all I have to tell you just now. I hope you don't mind the mistakes but I had no one to help me and I was in a hurry. I don't know why. I suppose they all send their love.

From Willie

The many ways in which life was complicated by World War II are plainly described in this series of letters between LES SULLIVAN, *who was serving in the RAAF, and his parents in Clybucca, near Kempsey, NSW. Les's grandmother Agnes bought the family farm in 1908. By 1943, however, Les's father, Harold, was forced to sell up and move to the city to find work to support his family. Ironically, Harold was unable to sell the farm on the open market because of price control regulations, which were meant to ensure no one profiteered from families affected by the war. It was leased, and later sold to its tenant.*

Despite Les's fears of evil city life, the family's move to Sydney was happy and prosperous. Harold rented a house in Bankstown, found work and eventually bought two adjacent blocks and built a family home on them in 1948. Les's sisters were soon employed, press-ganged into the war effort by manpower controls, and adapted easily to Sydney life. His younger brothers continued at school. After the war, Les became a teacher, and counted a young John Howard among his Year 3 students at Earlwood Primary School in

1948. He later graduated with an arts degree at Sydney University and returned to the RAAF in 1952, this time at the rank of flight lieutenant, and stayed there until retirement in 1974. Les's father died in 1956 and his mother, Nina, stayed in the Bankstown home until she died, aged 82, in 1980. The hardships of the war are long behind Les and his four siblings. Now, they count twelve children and eighteen grandchildren between them. Les, who contributed these letters, now lives at Pambula Beach on the NSW south coast.

1943
JULY 26
CLYBUCCA VIA KEMPSEY, NSW

My Dear Son,

I may as well tell you that your mother and I are thinking of leaving the farm. I am finding the work increasingly difficult with my old knee injury, which is why I would never allow you to play football. In the interests of Beryl and Mona who are now in their teens with no job prospects here except pulling cows' teats and of John who will be starting high school next year, and of Alan, we have decided to move to Sydney. While I am not keen on it in principle as it will be a big sacrifice, we hope and pray that it will be to the ultimate benefit of our children.

These 44 acres aren't enough to support a big family and our children will eventually have to leave home and this district to find work, just as you have done.

Your Loving Dad

1943
AUGUST 3
NO I ENGINEERING SCHOOL, RAAF
MELBOURNE

Dear Dad, Mum and Kids,

I am very sorry to hear that there may not be a farm to go home to on my next leave but with the way you are situated, I suppose it's the right decision.

With no end in sight to this war and the housing situation in Sydney, it may be impossible to find another comfortable home in these uncertain times.

While I would like to see the girls in good jobs, I would never want to see them on their own in Sydney as I have heard too much of what happens to inexperienced country girls in the city when their parents can't supervise them. It's a big risk so make sure you are completely satisfied, as the decision will affect all our lives. You would not want to end up drifting from one job to another, like so many do.

Your Loving Son,
Les

1943
SEPTEMBER 30
CLYBUCCA

My Dear Son,

I have just returned from a trip to Sydney in search of a house and a job and have never worried so much in all my life. It was a cow of a trip both ways on trains crowded with troops, so I had no sleep. I found a nice brick cottage in Lakemba for £1,175 but it was tenanted and I would not have been able to get the tenant out, and even if I could the owner would want "key money".

Finally I found a cottage in Bankstown, or at least half a house, as the owner wanted one room for herself. So with nothing better in view I took it. People have told me that I have done the impossible – rent a house in Sydney – but also that we will never want to go back to the country.

Because of Manpower Controls, I had to find a job connected with primary industry, so I looked up an old friend in the Producers' Distributing Society who is a foreman.

Because of my leg he offered me a job nailing up cases for a start and said that if I showed initiative I would soon be put up as they need men of my class and experience. He could also give the girls employment and they are thrilled at the prospect.

So there it is my boy. It will be a different life and work but will be better than this 14 hours a day, seven days a week, 52 weeks a year grind. I had the trip on your birthday gift which was a great help.

Your Loving Dad

1943
OCTOBER 4
RAAF MELBOURNE

Dear Mum and Dad and Kids,

I am glad to hear that you succeeded in the two miracles of getting a job and accommodation.

Be careful about the sort of job the girls get as some of those factory workers can be pretty rough, and having lived all their lives in the country, they could be in for some shocks. My year in the RAAF has opened my eyes to the things that go on in cities.

I will try and get leave before the sale, but don't want to be there to see everything connected with our lives, sold.

Your loving Son and Brother,
Les

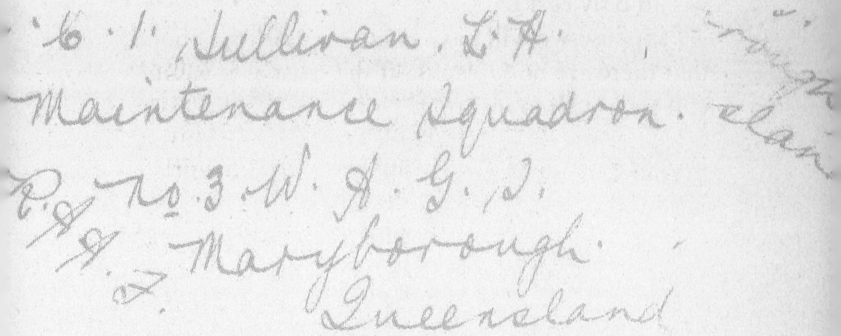

1943
OCTOBER 18
CLYBUCCA

My Dear Son,

We have decided to lease the farm, not sell it in case the move doesn't work out and also because of Price Control, we would not get what it is worth.

The successful tenderer offered us £4 for the 44 acres for three years which will bring in £176 per year. Everyone says he is an honest and hard worker.

Dad has been to Kempsey to see the police about an extra petrol ration for the drive to Sydney as we only get five gallons a month and will need about 20 gallons.

He also saw a removalist who quoted £20 just to pack our furniture and put it on the train but it may be weeks before it leaves because of war priorities.

So he enquired about sending it by sea on the 'Arakoon' where it would be loaded last on top of the other cargo and not be knocked around, but would only cost £8.

I suppose we will have to take the risk and hope that there are no Jap subs off the coast as it would cost too much to insure it.

Your Loving Mother

1943
NOVEMBER 10
CLYBUCCA

My Dear Son,

Our clearance sale on Saturday was a corker and half the Macleay must have been there. All the house paddock was full of cars with a lot more parked on the roadside.

I cooked a big piece of corned round and made six loaves of sandwiches and buttered a tin of Saos. All our milkers sold for record prices from £12 to £17 5 shillings for 'Princess'. The bull and both draught horses also brought good prices and our flood boat, for which we paid £4 10 shillings, went for £12. Beryl's tea set sold for thirteen and six and Alan's scooter, for £1 15 shillings.

Dad was like a dog with two tails at such a good result and because we had sold everything we offered. So now all we have left is ourselves and what we stand up in, and our furniture which is being packed today.

We have heard that there will be a big crowd at our send off in Clybucca Hall next Saturday night and wish you could be here for it.

Your loving Mother

Twin sisters VIOLET *and* DAISY WATT *penned this quick letter to their neighbour Margaret Bradshaw after the birth of her second child, Edward. Margaret's first child, Beverley (mother and daughter pictured), who was ten at the time, came and told Violet and Daisy the good news. The twin sisters lived next door to the Bradshaws on Eastbourne Road in Sydney's Darling Point.*

Beverley, who contributed this letter, now has an adult daughter of her own, Catriona, and lives in Sunshine Beach, southeast Queensland. Her brother, Edward, is fifty and lives in East Kilara, Sydney.

1951
1 EASTFIELDS,
EASTBOURNE RD
DARLING POINT
S. PETER AND S. PAUL

My dearest Margaret,

Beverley came to the door this morning in great excitement to say 'Mummy had the baby yesterday morning at half past six!' She does not seem so far to connect it with being a brother! I'm not surprised, are you?

We are so glad it is a boy as you wanted it to be! Beverley says we cannot come to see you until after Monday, so we shall come one day next week, if all's well.

About its present, we shall not bring it to the Hospital because it will only give you more to bring home, we shall have it waiting here for you. It is a purely utilitarian present, because in these grim days, useful presents are the best, don't you think so? Violet said you were looking particularly well on Wednesday afternoon when she saw you. You must have decided to have the baby in a hurry! Violet said she wondered when she saw the place shut up yesterday morning if you had already gone to Hospital, but I'm afraid I didn't even think of a baby arriving so soon!

Heartiest congratulations! We are so very glad it is a boy.

We shall be looking forward to seeing you next week, and then I suppose you will be coming home soon after that, so we shall see Edward then. (Are you going to keep to Edward or abbreviate it?)

With our love and prayers,
Violet & Daisy

In September 1960, PETER BURKE *and* JAN, *his bride of three weeks, both in their mid-twenties, set off from England as '£10 Pommie migrants' to Australia aboard the ageing SS Strathaird. As they*

steamed toward Fremantle the Burkes caught their first glimpse of Australia and were impressed. 'It was just like the best garden suburb you know, transplanted into a Mediterranean climate,' Peter wrote to his mother. However, their next stop, Melbourne, failed to impress. ('We drove for half an hour through the most dingy forlorn suburbs, and I couldn't help thinking what you said, Pop, about Melbourne being like Manchester!') The couple only stayed two weeks in the hostel hut in Footscray assigned to them by Immigration before renting their own apartment in Glen Iris. Although happy in Melbourne, they eventually decided to move to Sydney and in 1972 took out Australian citizenship. Jan's twin sister Pat (now Pat Downe) and her mother Vi Godley joined them in Australia, as did Peter's mother Johanna Burke, who kept all the letters her son wrote home to her and her husband in Twickenham, England. The couple, who raised their two sons, Ashley, 35, and Nick, 32, in their St Ives home, enjoyed 41 happy years of marriage in this country before Jan succumbed to cancer on Australia Day, 2002.

1960
PERTH
Oct 12

Dearest Mum & Dad,

Now it's Wed. 4pm and we've just rounded the SW tip of Australia, by Albany, and are in the Bight, which has a similar reputation to Biscay. Fortunately it is at present perfect, sun has shone all day, and the sea is calm, although we are rolling in the usual quite heavy swell, which doesn't bother us. We are sprawling on 'A' deck, listening to light music from Radio Perth, with the albatrosses gliding all round us. – but don't get too overawed – they are exactly like seagulls, only with a wingspan of about 6ft!

Now about Perth! No country could wish for a better city to display as a first impression to newcomers. We were tremendously impressed and so were most other people except some Aussies incl. Joan from Melbourne! Peter and Robert, the two Queenslanders, had never been outside their own state, and they really opened their eyes! Fortunately I got up at 6.30, when our steward brought in the tea, slipped on some clothes, and dashed up to 'A' deck. It was one of those beautiful crisp clear mornings, cold, with no cloud in the sky, where one really has to rub one's hands to keep warm; and there, in the distance, was our first glimpse of Australia! I dashed down, got Jan, and also put something warmer on, and we watched the approaches to Freemantle.

However, the ship stopped for the authorities to get on, and we couldn't dock before they had seen everyone. The previous day we had had the most farcical medical muster, where everyone had to file past that joke doctor, and he was supposed to see, without even looking at us, whether we had smallpox or not. I doubt if he would have noticed if we had a limb hanging off with leprosy, let alone smallpox! We also had to fill in a Press and TV questionnaire as they always interview people of interest. I said we shouldn't have too much publicity lest the stock exchange be completely swamped with the rush of business on the news that Burke has arrived!

At 10am we boarded our bus, equipped with loudspeaker so that the driver could give a commentary. We drove out to the suburbs of Freemantle, along the estuary of the Swan River. I just don't know where to begin! It was just like the best garden suburb you know, transplanted into Mediterranean climate. Even this is quite inadequate, as the houses are different from English, and the vegetation is totally unique. The streets, which were all very clean, with excellent surfaces, are all lined with trees – not monsters, but small gum trees and, in places, 'flame trees'. These had no leaves yet but only bunches of red blossoms shaped just like fingers of flame. Also palm trees of various sorts, but no cactus.

The houses were an absolute dream; almost entirely bungalows. Each one was detached, and never the same as the next. The roofs were tiled in the most gorgeous colours – royal blue, yellow, blue and black, and blue and mauve or red and yellow. The bricks were also of various pastel shades. The angles of the roofs are all big i.e. gentle sloping and with lots of little porticos, etc. They all have verandas, and look very clean and shiny. The gardens were all 'open plan', with lawns sloping down to the streets . . . I would hate 'open plan' in London, but here it's just like one huge park, so it doesn't matter. Land with a good view can cost anything from Australian £2600 and the house another £3000 upwards. I reckon one could get a nice new home in a fair position for Australian £5000. Less if you built it yourself.

We really have made some good friends and contacts, and I must tell you about some of them; Peter, from Qld is an awfully nice chap. He is 24, and works for the Bank of NSW. His father is bank manager in charge of all the relief staff for Qld. Peter has been 26 months in Port Moresby, New Guinea. He has a very ready sense of humour and a very dry drawl. A typical expression which came out last night was, instead of 'I was taking this girl out,' 'I was operating this doll.' He does not drink or smoke and has just been round the world, having saved £1300 in 2 years! His friend Robert is also a thoroughly nice upright chap – a grazier from W. Qld. Then there is the Small family – 4 of them have just been round the world! He has a brother in Real Estate. He asked me to jot down my qualifications for him and then ring him up. He thinks I may be just the type his brother is looking for. He has a flourishing branch in Qld, and has just built an £80,000 bridge to one of the islands. [This was Bruce Small, developer and future mayor of the Gold Coast, and the bridge was the Bribie Island bridge.]

Jan's Mum wrote that Rosemary C [the new bride of a fellow I knew in England who was on the ship with us] is very homesick. We asked her if this was true, and she said that at times she felt terribly bad. Jan has been extremely good in this respect and although she feels unhappy when she thinks that her Mum is lonely at home on her own, she has not had any real pangs of homesickness, and is otherwise fighting fit and rarin' to go when we arrive, looking forward to everything, and as game as they make 'em!

Must close now, so all our love, take it easy, drive carefully and keep up the non-smoking . . . Pete & Jan.

Melbourne
October 19, 1960

Dearest Mum & Pop,

Action stations at last! We docked in Melbourne at midnight, and were first woken up by an officers' party in the next cabin, as the Strathmore was alongside. Having shut them up, we next woke up to see the immigration people at 7am, up on 'B' deck. It was raining, cold and miserable outside and we both had that feeling in our stomachs . . . They didn't have a hostel (place) for us as they thought we were getting off in Perth! But they had your mail! Then breakfast, and saying goodbye to everyone including the West Indian cricketers with whom we have exercised each morning before breakfast for the past five weeks. [This was the team of the historic 1960 Test series, including Garfield Sobers, West Hall, and Rohan Kanhai.] Then off the old tub with mixed feelings, into the customs shed, where the only thing of interest to the officials were the 2 oranges the steward had given us that morning.

Then out to the bus that was to take us to Brooklyn hostel, Footscray – a name that will be for ever embedded in our minds. We drove for half an hour through the most dingy forlorn suburbs, and I couldn't help thinking what you said, Pop, about Melbourne being like Manchester!

The hostel is a camp of Nissen huts, painted bright blue and white, with one large canteen building. Don't think that we were feeling at all depressed – we were joking and laughing the whole time, and when we arrived, said that it was 'just like home!'

There were 2 busloads of us, and after a very pleasant talk from the warden, we were shown to our 'flatette'. This consisted of 1/12 of a Nissen hut, measuring 12ft x 9ft. A folding settee-bed and 2 old cupboards. In the corner a bucket with 2 brooms and dustpan, and also a footgrate. We just laughed! I put the footgrate outside the door, whereupon a ginger-haired, befreckled woman who had been cynically watching the arrival of us honeymooners to the lovenest came over and advised us, in tones of a very experienced sage, not to leave the footgrate outside the door, as we'd never see it again!

We nearly died when we heard that the average stay here is 14 months – some people stay 5 years. They save up money and then go back to the UK and tell you what a rotten place Australia is! Some of them have never been out of Melbourne, and I am sure many have seldom been even to the city!

Next door to our field of Nissen huts is an abattoir, and the smell is appalling! The land is flat, with factories all round. It is ghastly, but for some of these people, they're well off. All have TV masts, and the road is full of cars! The women do nothing all day, but gossip – no cooking, very little cleaning, and everything is laid on. Dad earns good money. Some do try to get out but it's difficult. It cost £4 12 shillings for a man, £4 for a woman and about £2 for each child, so for a family with 2 kids, Dad might earn £25, and pay £12 for full board, and most of the rest can be saved. Some do save up about £5000. Others want to get out, but find themselves caught in a vicious circle. The work is on this side of town, but without a car, they can't buy a house. To buy the house they want, it's too far from their work, so they stay!

On our cupboard was a tray with cutlery, 2 mugs and a toilet roll! We had to trot over to the canteen with cups and cutlery and help ourselves to the grub – not bad and fairly wholesome well-cooked grub. You also get a sink plug supplied, and take this with you to wash – they can't leave anything as it just gets stolen. People leave the canteen with mountains of bread; the sugar is always empty, and I saw a woman today filling a thermos the size of a bucket with tea – hiding it under her coat – can you imagine!

After lunch we went straight back to the city via the appalling bus service. We got our money and a cheque book each. Then to a chemist where we took out our health insurance, covering us against everything except dental and optical. Cost £5 six shillings per quarter for both of us – not each! Compare this to 9/11 each per week at home! Then we had a look at the shops, and had some 'English tea'. The weather was bitterly cold and raining on and off. By that time we had to get back for 'tea' i.e. supper. Determined not to stay there the evening, I phoned Kevin & Barbara. They were expecting us and said we should come over. So back to town (an hour by bus!) and Kevin met us at the GPO. Charming couple, been married 1 year, and just expecting their 1st baby. Couldn't do enough for us. Took us out to their house in Kew and we had a lovely evening, and he ran us all the way back. They are taking us out on Sunday to the National Park where all the native animals are supposed to roam wild. Kevin says the koalas and kangaroos are quite shiny from such frequent stroking, but they still pretend they're wild!

Next day we bought a car! A 1948 Hillman Minx for £225. I hope I've done the right thing!

All our love,
Pete & Jan

DR GIOVANNI ANDREONI *(pictured overleaf), a teacher and writer from Grosetto, Italy, migrated to Australia in 1962, but it wasn't until 1974, at the height of the Whitlam era, that he considered taking out Australian citizenship. In this translated letter to his mother, Maria Bertocci Andreoni, he enthuses about Whitlam's vision to end 'assimilation' and 'build a new Australia'. Dr Andreoni, who went on to head the Italian department at the University of New England in Armidale, NSW, married an Australian, Helen Cook. The couple have two adult children, Marco, who is living in Japan, and Francesca, who lives in Sydney.*

1974
2 January

Mother,

I have decided to become an Australian citizen. 'Tempus fugit' and I don't want to miss the chance of participating in the rebirth of this vast and beautiful land.

For many years the detached observer within ruled my life finding faults and ridiculing colonial Australia. It was indeed an easy task! At the theatre one had to stand up and be afflicted by the sound of 'God Save the Queen'. In every public building small and large effigies of Elizabeth II harrowed the poor visitor. I don't mind the photos as much as the portraits of Her Majesty in regal attire – her selection of artists is as pedestrian as her choice of hats.

You know all this from my letters, full as they are of humorous and not so humorous details illustrating the dullness of colonial Australia. You also know I was trying to hide from you my anguish at the realisation that my only function was to serve and be grateful. At the University I am constantly reminded that, being a wog, I have overstepped the mark by working there.

No reasonable person can blame me for not wishing to be assimilated. Assimilation is the dehumanising scheme of colonial Australia. Migrants will be educated into accepting proper roles assigned to them by their masters: wogs and dagos can grow vegetables and sell fish. Huns work as mechanics, blacks as farm hands. Their children will soon forget the old culture and think and act like happy little Australians.

What a squalid and destructive policy.

Well a huge man stood up in Parliament, his name is Gough Whitlam, and behind him there is an unruly mob of dreamers and reformers. Down with assimilation – they shout – let us accept and respect each other for what we are, let's build the new Australia together.

Now Mother, control yourself, I know you are going to quote 'il vecchio Machiavelli'. I too remember his words; that reformers will always come to grief, because they face an unrelenting opposition from all those who benefited from the old system, and only lukewarm support from those who might benefit from the new order. I am old enough to be able to survive the possible failure of this dream of 'Egalite, Fraternite, Liberte'. But I am also young enough to feel the elation of these Promethean days. It is grand to partake of such historical events.

Write to me soon. I must know what you think.

I miss you.
Giovanni.

WINIFRED WATSON *was a spirited woman, and lifelong supporter of the Liberal Party. So when Gough Whitlam's prime ministership started to flounder in 1974 amid high inflation and endemic strikes, her response, as articulated in these letters to her daughter and son-in-law in London, was emphatic. In the election that followed Whitlam's dismissal, she worked for the Liberal campaign in Burnie, Tasmania. She met her hero, Malcolm Fraser, in 1977, while he was prime minister (pictured). Winifred died in 1983, aged 77. These letters were submitted by her daughter Marilyn Quirk, who lives in Penguin, Tasmania.*

1974
23 July
BURNIE, TASMANIA.

Dear Marilyn and Trevor,

Now about Gough – he has gone pretty subdued lately. Inflation is up again to 16%, everyone is screaming. He's going to rise the postage up to 10 cents; phone rental increase up to $75.00; increase taxation and sales tax. Things are in an awful mess and don't be surprised when you return if the money hasn't been devalued.

We have got a transport workers' strike on now. Poor old Tasmania is having a bad go.

I rang up Peter to tell him that you had seen his relatives. He was was very worried about the fate of his parents in Cyprus as his father works at the airport which was bombed and he was trying to get some news. They had put a telex through but the airport was not answering. Looks as if your whole Greece/Cyprus visit will have to be called off.

Don't get caught up with any bombing etc. Yes we are lucky to be away from it, but if Gough keeps on like he is, someone might put a bomb under him.

Mum

1974
6 August
BURNIE, TASMANIA.

Dear Marilyn and Trevor,

I'm sending you today's paper so that you can read about Gough. He's gone stone mad, and at the University they say the inflation will be up to 25 per cent next year. I notice everything is just bounding up. The chickens have gone up a dollar and everything looks too dear to buy.

They are having their joint sitting of the two houses of Parliament today and they are on TV. There is no doubt Gough thinks he's God's gift to the nation. I reckon the Libs only have to keep quiet and they will hang themselves soon. Everyone is commenting on it.

You know there is an awful strike on and we are going to be cut off from the mainland, even by air. It's about time they did something about the unions. I was talking to that woman down the lane (you know her husband rides to work on a bike), and she was telling me that her husband is off from work tomorrow – the first time for 25 years.

Mum

1974
28 August
BURNIE, TASMANIA.

Dear Marilyn and Trevor,

I am making this our last letter to you people as if you get back to London in three weeks' time you will probably be off again and any further letters will miss you. Also we seem to be having postal strikes on and off and I don't know how long this is going to take to get to you.

Things have really gone bad here. Mr Mundy, who is now head of the Communist Party, has made it public that he intends calling out all the workers in a 'spring offensive'. We've got strikes, strikes and more strikes going now. The Paper Mill nearly closed, and Goliath Cement is in the process of closing down, and the chip industry too. The town only has two days of petrol left. I don't know if it's the transport drivers, or the oil drivers or both. The papers all reckon the country is in a state of anarchy, and it is.

We never hear of Mr [Frank] Crean these days. I heard he is going to be given another post. Dr Cairns seems to have taken over. We haven't heard from Gough for quite a while and everyone was saying he was going to resign but he denied it and spoke to the nation. All his puff has gone out of him. Anyway, before you book (air fares), read the papers as it may coincide with Mr Mundy's offensive and you may get stranded.

Tell Trev he had better get a haircut before he gets to Singapore as they won't let any long-haired people in there, did you know?

Mum

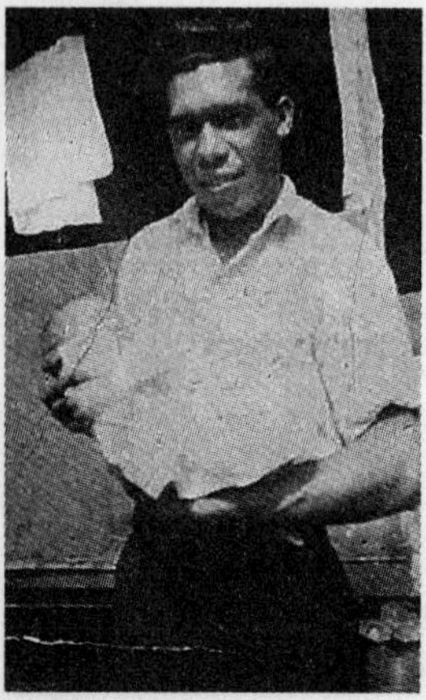

FRANK GOODA *(pictured with his eldest son Angus) wrote this letter to his daughter Judith in Mackay in 1970. He was 42 and was recovering from a serious accident two years earlier on a construction site at the wharf of Port Alma just south of Rockhampton in which he had suffered severe internal injuries. As a young Aboriginal boy growing up in Baralabra, west of Rockhampton, Frank had taught himself to read and write. He believed education was the key to Aboriginal advancement, and could quote the verse of Henry Lawson and sing the songs of Hank Williams Snr. Frank, who had nine children, died eight years after writing this letter, which was contributed by his daughter Judith Devine of Rockhampton.*

1970
110 WEST STREET
ROCKHAMPTON
4th August

Darling Judith
Greetings and Salutations Honey. It was good to hear you on the phone tonight if only for a few words. Glad you like it up there and I hope you keep on enjoying things there. Everyone seems to be fine. Stacy Louise (that's Angus and Rhonda's baby) is in the hospital with the wog. As I told you on the phone I haven't had a hard drink for six weeks now and I also gave up bex and I haven't been away from the hospital it seems there a couple of tubes from the kidneys to the bladder is not functioning properly I've got to see a doctor for the result of all the tests I've had. But I am real good now. Maybe all the alcohol and bex is out of my system now. So much for our ills now for something brighter. Cathy is turning into a human talking machine she talks non stop during her waking hours. I can't put here what all she says but she swears every time the postman calls and they're no letters from you. 'That ____ Judy never writes to me'.

Michael went down to Brisbane last week with the cadets for a fortnight. Mackie went down to Bundaberg last weekend to play football and had a wonderful time. Deano's team won the Premiership last week. And they are holding a Barbeque for all the Mothers on Wednesday night. Bimbo is real fine he's working from 9am to 7pm in the Parcel Office now. Paul is the same. He played the wag one day last week. We came home from town and there he was under the house. Angus and Rhonda are staying here and are both real good. Evelyn, Jennifer, Rhonda and her baby were here for the day last week. They came down for a new truck for Colin. They said Mrs Cross wants you to write to her. Kay Kerr comes round here a lot Doug kicked her out and put their little boys in the St George Home out at Parkhurst. The Kemps are all the same. We don't go down there very often. Billy bought a 60 Holden for $100 you can imagine what it's like for that price. Oil runs out of every where. The mufflers fall off, runs on three cylinders but Bill gets it there. Janet and Siggy got a house like ours on the western side of the Range. Margie is still the same.

Jackie Hopes (Robyn's Dad) passed away. It seems he contacted that Hong Cong flu and it wouldn't break and caused a clot on his brain. We didn't find out until after the funeral. We all the boys went to the show. I went for half a day Cathy had the measles so we couldn't go out much. Your Mother and I won the feature double on Divide and Rule and Cashadeo of $349. So we were able to buy all the boys new outfits. We've been picking up a few dollars nearly every week. Helping us along quite a bit.

Well Darling that is all I can think of to tell you for now so I'll say bye bye. With lots of love to you from your,

Loving Dad, Mum and the Boys

P.S. Give Bob our best regards and try and come up to visit us for some weekend. Dad. Lots of kisses from Cathy.

VERA McDOUGALL *was 82 and living alone on a wheat and sheep property near the Grampians in the Western District of Victoria when she wrote these letters to her granddaughter, Fiona Ryan (pictured with Vera), a teacher in Alice Springs. Vera's son Ray and his daughter Sue lived nearby, while Vera's daughter Helen and her husband Frank (Fiona's parents) lived in Ballarat, as did their other daughter, Marcia. Vera's husband had died in 1970 and although still very active Vera was struggling to live on her own and would spend periods of time at Helen and Frank's in Ballarat. She never did go into the retirement village, but died at the age of 87 after moving permanently to Ballarat. This letter was contributed by Fiona Ryan, who now lives in Semaphore in South Australia and is a school counsellor in Port Adelaide.*

27/2/80
'ROSEVALE'
MAROONA 3290

My Dear Fiona,

I was so pleased to get your letter. Things have been happening here the last few days.

We have had another dust stormy day, and of course you would have heard about the disastrous fires – it is heart breaking to read about and everyone knows someone who has been affected. The country is so bare – as your grandfather used to say 'you could whip a flea from one end of a paddock to the other'. That expression always amused me.

But I have 'had it' and am leaving the dust, so tomorrow I will go to Ballarat when Ray brings Sue home. I intended to stay here and see the hot weather out now that I have an air conditioner, but I am only another worry for Ray, if a fire happens to come this way.

Yesterday Ray and Bruce and two men from Ararat were cutting down some of the old pine plantation. Ray ran in to tell me that one of the men had cut off his little finger and Bruce had rushed him to Ararat Hospital. The poor man was in terrific pain and Ray was most upset. He immediately rang Roy Richards to see if the man was covered by the farm insurance. Roy assured him that he was – so that was a blessing for all concerned.

Here is an anecdote to give you a smile. I met Charlie Phillips in Ararat last week. He was an old admirer of mine 60 years ago but as J. K. used to say 'old soup is easily warmed up!' Well he was very effusive and said he supposed I knew his wife had died recently and he has come back to live in Ararat and gave me his address!! Ray was very amused. Now that might solve (or make) all our problems.

I must away. Sue read your letter and no doubt will write to you.

I'm afraid the drought is getting her down.

Love From Gran

3/5/80
'ROSEVALE'
MAROONA 3290

My Dear Fiona,

Your mum's birthday, and she was going out to a luncheon and then dinner tonight. I can't keep up with their social life.

Last Sunday when I was in Ballarat your mum and dad went out to lunch. As it was a nice day, I pottered about in the back garden. The back gate was open, and I heard (and saw) a man waving his arms and shouting – down the middle of the street. When he passed the gate, I went out to see what he was shouting at, and there was only a woman down the end of the street going for her life. To my horror he returned and saw me peering at him. I can tell you I have never moved so quickly for years.

I had to find the back door key, unlock it and hurriedly lock myself in. Then I sat in the lounge. I knew when your mum and dad came home they wouldn't find the back door key but would come round to the front door and I would let them in. But it didn't work out that way. Hearing a noise I went out to open the back door, saw the car in the garage and waited for them to come in the front. I couldn't understand what was keeping them. Then I heard a noise in the bedroom. I walked towards it and met your mum in blouse and panty hose – she had taken off her skirt and your dad had pushed her through your window. They were both very cross at being locked out of their own home and I wasn't too popular for a while. Incidentally the old fellow is from Lakeside and often comes round the block shouting out, but quite harmless – how was I to know?

Sue is home this weekend as usual. She bought the bad news that Paddles Factory are in a bad way and a lot are being retrenched and may even close down. Poor Sue she is in a state.

Winter is just around the corner and I am not looking forward to it.

Love From Gran

Forgot to tell you that last Saturday when I was in Ballarat, Marcia came home. We all sat over the dinner table till 12.30am. Our discussion was 'Marriage' versus 'Living Together' – no need to tell you what role Marcia took. Your mother 'sat on the fence' and your father agreed with me sometimes and with Marcia sometimes. We all agreed that a happy marriage is an institution which cannot be bettered, but Marcia has doubts about how to obtain the 'happy' part of it!

I hope you enjoyed your weekend in Tennant Creek and I look forward to hearing all about it.

Gran

Sunday October 1980
'ROSEVALE'
MAROONA 3290

My Dear Fiona,

Thankyou for the card from Ayers Rock. Sue has been sick and couldn't come over this weekend so I stayed alone last night. I have the phone at my bedside now so that makes me feel safer, but Ray only worries.

I went to the Hamilton Races with Ray on Friday and had 4 wins and 1 2nd. It was a perfect Spring day and I thoroughly enjoyed the outing. A fortnight ago I went to the Minyip Races, so I am enjoying going round the country. On Tuesday your mother is coming up and she is taking me to the Retirement Village in Ararat for a fortnight's holiday to see how I like it. I feel the time is approaching when I must make a move. I fell over last week – a giddy turn and I have had a couple of nasty incidents which you will probably laugh at.

Firstly, I always keep a pair of shoes on the side verandah if I want to go out in the garden. I was putting on a shoe when a mouse ran out of it and ran up my leg!! Thank goodness I had tights (pantyhose) on!!!

Never-the-less the shock was so severe and I haven't yet recovered. Then yesterday I was hanging some clothes on the line and before I realised it, I was covered in little ants – I was standing on an ant nest, and they are very busy for this fine weather. The little beasts were nipping me from top to toe – and I didn't have panty hose on! I rushed inside (as quickly as I can go) stripped and got under the shower but for a few hours I looked as if I had measles. Thank heaven the marks soon disappeared – but did you realise little ants bite? What if it had been bull ants?

After all that don't you think it's a good idea to leave this place to the mice and ants?

Please write to me next week
@ Retirement Village
McGibbony Street
Ararat 3377

Think of me
Love From Gran

Letters from Far Away

Playwright DAVID WILLIAMSON *(pictured overleaf with his wife Kristin) was the better for wine when he wrote this warm response to New York-based novelist Peter Carey, who had telephoned him a few days earlier. Although the letter talks about moving to Port Douglas, Williamson found his 'paradise' at Noosa Heads. This letter is held in the National Library of Australia (MS 7378/381). It is printed with permission of David Williamson, of Sunshine Beach, Queensland.*

10 JUNE 1993

Dear Peter,

Re: Life, The Meaning Thereof, and Other Profundities.

It was so good to hear you this morning on the phone, if for no other reason than to remind us both what a dear and valued friend you are. (I could never say this verbally which is why the fax is sometimes such a wonderful invention.) Frankly both Kristin and I were a little worried and guilty that we didn't respond in a more open and communicative way, getting bogged down in a wealth of platitudes, self-promotional news bulletins, and other inanities. The truth is that we were both deeply touched, both that you phoned up out of the blue and that you felt such an obvious and endearing nostalgia for things Australian. The Spanish extroversion reminding you of home, and the Australian Ambassador being so warm and friendly seemed to carry to us a barely disguised subtextual message that you hadn't yet managed to throw off the last vestiges of that deep-rooted and irrational tribalism which is so much a part of our own psyche.

As I get older the love of this country, like your own, starts to focus more and more on the landscapes. I have a dream of living in a beautiful Australian environment far out of Sydney and to the north.

Possibly in the area of Port Douglas which I think is one of the earth's most beautiful regions. I find increasingly that the prickly ambition, which drove me so hard in my earlier years, is fading, and I just want to wander amongst tropical plants and marvel at my luck that one sperm out of millions hit the egg and gave me the chance, albeit briefly, to marvel at the interlocking weave of life forms around me. This condition is sometimes called wisdom, more often senility. I am still doing the project for [Robert] Altman, my play is working wonderfully, but I couldn't really give a f... I still want to keep writing plays, but in a leisurely and considered way that allows time for thinking, reading, reflection and tropical splendour. We can't of course move until Rory is finished at school, but the thought is there in both my own and Kristin's mind with a strength that indicates that it's not just a geriatric fantasy.

If you and Alison [Summers] ever get to the point where the tawdry baubles of ambition cease to beguile, we should settle within visiting distance of each other somewhere up there and enjoy the incomparable landscapes and each other's company. We did enjoy the time when you were only a stone's throw away in Louisa Road, and this is a wonderful country, something that as my brain cells deplete becomes more and more obvious to me. I sometimes feel as if a benevolent but mischievous god gave our forefathers the use of a land they tricked up as hellish, then slowly revealed to us, their descendants, that in fact we had been given Paradise. If you think I'm off my nut and blind drunk (I am), wait until you see Far North Queensland.

Thanks again for the call. We miss you all a lot.

DW.

ERIC DOYLE *wrote this homesick letter to his parents from boarding school in 1905. This and many other Doyle family letters were found by journalist Geoff Walker under a house in Lemon Tree Passage, NSW. In 1917, as an artillery officer in World War I, Eric was awarded the Military Cross. An official letter was sent to inform his parents. Eric's father, Dr Doyle, immediately wrote to his son: 'I got home and told Mum that I had a wonderful letter and we two old people sat down and I read it to her and she wept tears of joyfulness, and as I did, thought it truly great and significant and wonderful – then we offered in our hearts fervent prayers of thankfulness that you were spared.' Several weeks later a telegram arrived informing them that Second-Lieutenant Eric Doyle MC had been killed in action at Flanders, even before Dr Doyle had written the letter to his son. Dr Doyle never recovered from the news, and turned to spiritualism in an attempt to communicate with his son.*

Armidale School
ARMIDALE
31/6/05

My Darling Dad,
I hope you are quite well.

I am very sorry I could not write to you yesterday and I hope you will forgive me as I was up in the sickroom with a bad cold as soon as I had finished writing to Mum.

I hope I will not have to go to this beastly school again as I am sick of it and I only wish I was home once more and I would give five years pocket money to be at home for five minutes.

I only wish it was twenty weeks from June as I feel like running away from this miserable hole. O Dad you don't know how I feel as it is beyond words and I only wish I could be taken away from here for I hate Armidale and everything in it, nobody to say good-night to. O I am terrible. I will go mad with joy when I see the old people once more and darling Barney. O do take me home. I pray you, as I think my heart will break here. If only I could see your faces again I would give a thousand pounds. The boys swear here and smoke and I pray you again take me away. I have no friend. I am alone. O take me home as quick as you can do! do! give notice as quick as you can to Mr Fisher do please. I cannot work proply? Why! I want to be home. Do ask mother to write to Mr Fisher if not will you Father. I say take heed of my words if you don't I will go crazy. Take me away at Michaelmas while there is yet time if not I will try and get ill and get home that way if you don't take heed of my words. Remember I am in second form for Latin. I am in first form for everything else.

I must close now.
I remain your ever, ever
loving Son,
Eric

P.S. God bless you all and remember my words.

jesty's Service.

WAR OFFICE

A. Doyle F.R.C.S.I.

Bungarra,

River Road

Milton, Brisbane,

Australia

FREDERICK ARMIDALE MARRIOTT *(pictured with his family), 38, sent this hurried letter home to Moreland, Ballarat, in October 1918. He was working as a mining engineer in southern Rhodesia (Zimbabwe), and had left his wife, Eveline, and their three children, Dorothy (9), Edward (7) and Phillip (3) in Australia. Nine days later he was dead as the Spanish flu epidemic swept the world. The third worst recorded plague in history, the epidemic lasted for 120 days, and took the lives of more than 21 million people worldwide, more than double the death toll of World War I. Africa was one of the worst hit regions, losing 1.3 million people. Australia lost 13,320 people. This letter was contributed by a great granddaughter of Frederick, Kate Welleman (née Marriott), of Point Lonsdale, Victoria.*

21.10.18
BUSHTICK MINE.

My darling Wife,
Just a hurried note. The Influenza epidemic is raging all over Africa. Everything is disorganised. Here 500 out of 600 natives are down, the Manager and many whites. I am in charge and trying to keep going, at same time feel pretty cheap. So hope that you are well, as soon as the P. Office can do it I'll send a cable, practically all business in Bulawayo is at a standstill. Burn this as soon as read in case of infection. Heaps of love to the kiddies and yourself.

Ever your loving husband,
Frederick A. Marriott

After writing this letter during the Depression, ALEX FITES *(pictured during WWII) spent a difficult year and a half searching for work, and ended up selling bags of fertiliser around Brisbane from the back of a hired horse and cart. In 1932, through nothing short of a miracle, according to his wife Alice, he found a job with the Dunlop Rubber Company. He worked as one of its commercial travellers for more than 30 years, retiring with a gold watch. He died in 1991, aged 80. Errol Flynn, meanwhile, soon found himself a world away from the Papuan copra plantations and under the bright lights of Hollywood, where he was to become one of the world's most famous actors. These letters were contributed by Mrs Alice Fites of Kedron, Brisbane.*

1931
SEPTEMBER 16
NEW FARM, BRISBANE

To E. T. Flynn Esq., C/o Messrs. Whitten Bros., Port Moresby, Papua

Dear Sir,

Owing to a reduction in staff, I have been thrown out of employment, after having been employed by Messrs. A.C.F. and Shirleys Fertilizers Ltd. for the last five years. Whilst in their employ I noticed a letter from you enquiring for tobacco fertilizer. It occurs to me that you may be looking for some labour this season, and if so I should be glad if you would give my case your consideration.

I have a fairly extensive knowledge of both fertilizers and spraying materials and am familiar with all types of spraying and dusting machines. My age at present is 20 and my weight is 10 stone. I am in good physical condition.

I have had no experience in practical tobacco growing, but have read up the subject and feel sure that I would be as capable as the next man in adapting myself to any class of work.

I have had some experience in book keeping and considerable experience in commercial practices, so would be perfectly capable of keeping returns and statistics on the farm in addition to manual labour. Trusting you will give my application your favourable consideration.

Yours faithfully,
A Fites
P. S. Copies of References enclosed.

OCTOBER 3, 1931
Laloki Plantation, Papua,

TO MR A. FITES, BRISBANE.

Dear Mr Fites,

Your letter of the 16th September is to hand. I regret to have to inform you that there is no opportunity for you up here. I am planting 15 acres of tobacco mainly as an experiment and the uncertainty of the venture makes it imperative that the cost of production should be as light as possible and I am afraid that in its present stage it would not justify the employment of another white hand.

I should like to have had an opportunity to help you.

Yours faithfully,
Errol L. Flynn

GIVE EMPLOYMENT
— ASSIST —
NATIONAL RECOVERY

Vineyard owner and ham radio operator HURTLE HOBCROFT *(pictured) received this letter in 1948. It was the early days of radio and Hurtle was in radio contact with people all over Australia, and was even in communication with Charles Kingsford Smith on his record-breaking flight from America to Australia in 1928. Hurtle had met the author of the letter,* H. NICHOLSON, *fifteen years earlier when Nicholson had knocked on the door and asked for some food. It had been 1933 and the Depression was at its height. Swaggies on the road were a common sight in the Renmark area and, indeed, all over Australia. H. Nicholson never forgot the kindness shown him. He and Hurtle, who shared the love of radio, began corresponding after this letter, which only arrived at Hurtle's house thanks to the folk at the Renmark Post Office. The envelope was addressed thus:*

Mr ____________
Wireless Operator living at House in the angle of the road out of Renmark and the road to Wentworth, about 2 miles from Renmark
South Australia

This letter was contributed by Hurtle's son Rex Hobcroft, of Melville, Perth.

30 April 48.
Mr X
Wireless Operator
Junction of Renmark & Wentworth Rds
RENMARK. S.A.

Dear Sir,

Herein or hereby my promise to write to you after I had arrived in England. You will remember me as the tramp to whom you gave a breakfast about 15 years ago – the 'telegraph operator'.

Well as you will see I got to England as a stowaway from Fremantle and as you will probably understand from the exigencies of my position there I have not done much through those same exigences here, however, although progress has been very slow, I have still been able to think and have learned a great deal from a study of physics electrostatics etctera.

But I am writing now for a particular purpose, as recently I have heard of a wireless operator here by the name of Sam Woolley of Chesterfield Derbyshire – G8RQ is his call – who has among other remarkable achievements followed, by wireless, a ship from 'Charleston to Sydney' – I should have said in practically constant communication with same.

And so I thought of you probably being in the same spot and that you might like to try and contact him because from the newspaper account of his achievements I do really think that he is an expert of the experts. I do not know yet what wavelength he uses or any details but if I find out then I will let you know if you are interested and anyway that will be enough for the present until I hear from you.

H. Nicholson
Sunnyside Farm
Kempsey
Worcester
England

In 1958, KEN HUMPHREYS *echoed the experience of hundreds of Australians in the decades after World War II when he arrived in Papua New Guinea for a stint as a patrol officer. In effect, he was a public servant administered from Canberra. In reality, he couldn't have been further removed from life in the Australian capital. He was posted to Daru in the Western District and then Kiunga at the top of the Fly River. One of the jobs of patrol officers was to administer local police units and this is what Ken writes to his sister Cherryl about. Other jobs included social worker, magistrate, postmaster, agricultural adviser, wireless operator, anthropologist, coroner, treasury clerk and engineer. Australia administered Papua New Guinea until it gained its independence from the United Nations in 1975. Ken, who is pictured with his police staff in PNG, is now retired and lives in Caloundra, Queensland.*

c/- Sub-District Office
KIUNGA,
WESTERN DISTRICT
PAPUA.
10th October 1958.

Dear Cherryl,

I received your letter just before I left Daru and I was very pleased with it. Your writing was also good and it is no wonder you do well at school. I suppose you will be having exams pretty soon, and I know you will do well in them. I will give you some extra pocket money if you come top in the yearly exam. I think it would be worth $3 to you if you did that. Anyhow best of luck and don't flirt with too many boys.

The plane that I came up here on also brought a letter from Mum that was a bit late in getting to Daru, and I am very sorry to hear about her osteo-arthritis. Tell Mum that because I didn't get her letter sooner I hadn't put anything in my last letter about her back. I have had no more trouble with my back as yet.

By the time you get this letter my friend Jane will have left for Tasmania. I hope she enjoyed her stay with you and I want to thank you for all the work you did to the house. Mum told me all about it in her letters.

I hope our dog Lady did not jump on the bed like she used to do when I was home. Is Dad feeding Lady OK and not letting her jump on the seats of the Morris 1000. I'm sorry that the letter is not well typed as the typewriter has been playing up a bit, but we have just put in a new ribbon as you can see. The typewriter is very old as is everything else in KIUNGA.

The plane trip up was OK and took about 2 1/2 hours. We passed over the Fly River and landed on Lake Murray to meet the Patrol Officer who will be with me here. He is on patrol in Lake Murray. He is just like the film star, Aldo Ray, and his name is Brian McBride. I have a man staying with me who is an engineer and is here to look for an airstrip site. Since we got here we have been going out in the bush with surveying instruments. It was hard work as the country is all rain forest. We had to clear a lot of it so we could take measurements. I sweated a terrible lot, and drank a lot of suppora drink which is just like lemon drink.

I am living in a two man house with no plumbing. It is not too bad and we have a good view of the river as the house is up on a hill. There is another house but no one is living in it. I have Joseph the house boy with me. He needs a lot of teaching however. I sent one of the policemen out with a shotgun during the week and he brought back some big fat pigeons which make nice eating. There is a school here and it is funny to see the pupils playing cricket and swimming in the waterhole. There is one little fellow who has lost all the hair off his head and he wears a little laplap (or rami) which is like a towel wrapped around your tummy.

There are a lot of mossies and flies and every night it rains cats and dogs. I sleep under a net and go to sleep about 9 o'clock as we have no electric lights but use pressure lamps which are hard to read by. The river flow is fast and last Saturday I had a swim in the river but it was very muddy and I didn't stay in very long. I am typing this up in the office which has three rooms and is built of native material, but it is very cool. I will take a photo of it on the next reel. The sun is very hot and there are a few clouds in the sky. Last Saturday night the police called me out as a murderer had just come to give himself up. I put him in the prison as I have to wait for Brian to come back as I have no power to try him. As well as that the radio is out of order and we have no communication with Daru. We are expecting a boat any day now and then the plane comes in next Thursday and this letter will be on it. Every morning there is a crowd of natives outside the office waiting to see me, usually with their little troubles. Some people came in this week saying that a boy had died and his parents had kept him in the hut for a week before burying him. This is against the law and the Headman came in just now and I told him to stop the practice.

How is your piano coming along? I suppose Jane gave you some tips about it. Mum said she was bringing her violin up with her. Did you enjoy it? The natives up here are very small and the women wear grass skirts. There is a little village near KIUNGA where there are a few pigs but not many people. I am going to start to learn the MOTU language as it does not seem very difficult.

Love, Kent

JOOLEE EADIE-EDWARDS *went to New York in the 1960s to study acting and dance. She was working at the Australian News and Information Bureau as a typist during the day and studying at the Alvin Ailey Dance Company by night. In October 1962 the world held its breath for thirteen tense days as the Cuban missile crisis – the most dangerous moment of the Cold War – played itself out. Despite America's very real fears that the Soviet Union was planning a nuclear attack, the crisis was averted and Joolee was able to continue her Christmas shopping. The cape, a full-length number, red on one side and leopard skin on the other, was finished in due course with the help of Ves Harper, the dance company's costume designer, and was a big hit. Joolee went on to teach dance in Sydney and perform with the Margaret Barr Dance Drama Company.*

NEW YORK
23rd October, 1962

Dear Mum & Dad,

I had doubts about writing this to you because I suppose you'll worry but then you will worry anyhow so here goes: – so far all is well, but every one is on tender hooks and I suppose something could happen at any moment. By something I mean the eastern powers leaving the U.N. If this step is taken I think it would be best for me to return home but I haven't any money. So, if the eastern powers leave the U.N. could you please cancel my insurance policies and wire me the money and that way I may be able to get a plane out of New York. Of course if New York IS hit it won't be safe anywhere on the earth but I suppose I'd rather be home than here. I don't want to leave, it means not being able to come back again if things are clear and carrying on with my ambition. I'm just writing this in case, don't worry about it, I just want to know that if things start happening I'll have money to get out. Please God all will be well. If anything should happen here I know it will be quick and most probably easier for me than you. Meanwhile things go on as normal and I'm still doing my Xmas shopping. Tonight I go for a fitting of my cape. I am making it, Ves is helping me so that way it shouldn't cost too much.

I hope you don't mind me writing this to you. DON'T WORRY.

I'm not that worried – This is just in case.

Luv,

Joolee

xxx

MRS JULIAN CHAPMAN *arrived in Australia in March 1968 as a '£10 Pommie migrant' and applied to the Commonwealth Education Department for a job as a teacher in the Northern Territory. She was sent to Papunya in September 1968, shortly before the establishment of the School of Painting, whose celebrated artists brought a turning point in the appreciation of Aboriginal art around the world. After eighteen months at Papunya, Julian, who wrote home to her father and stepmother fortnightly, moved to a one-teacher school on a cattle station, still working with Aboriginal children. Julian, who is pictured with her Papunya school class, now lives in Port Macquarie, NSW.*

PAPUNYA
September 26th, 1968

Dear Both of You,

It seems hard to believe that I have been here over a week now. I'm beginning to get used to seeing dark faces everywhere which seemed so strange at first. Each face looks different now instead of them all being the same. I haven't got my own class yet as Geoff doesn't move to a new Settlement until next week. When he goes Michael will take the senior class and I will take over Michael's which is the class below. The discipline has to be strict otherwise the children get very out of hand. I am still standing in wonder that even though some of them have only known White Man a few years, they can understand so much English. They can speak and write it too but are too shy to speak unless they are forced to. They chatter amongst themselves in their own languages and giggle wildly when spoken to. A lot of pressure is put on them at home to believe anything a white teacher says is 'rubbish talk' which makes things rather difficult.

Today and tomorrow is school sports. Truckloads of children have been driven and camped overnight from five other Settlements, anything up to 300 miles away across sandy tracks in the desert. Actually it's not a desert as I would think of it because there is tufty spinnifex grass and clumps of purple and white everlasting flowers. Last week I went with David and Jan to the nearest high place which is called Papunya Hill, about ten miles away. We climbed the red rocks right to the top and could look back on our midget Settlement floating (almost) in a vast plain with a ridge of blue mountains in the distance. Looking the other way the mountains are nearer, but lines of them stretch away endlessly. We could see a lorry and trailer wending its way in a cloud of dust towards Western Australia. On the way back we got bogged in deep sand. We got out after 30 minutes with the help of a few Aborigines coming back to camp. I shall have to get a car I think and a sleeping bag so that I can travel around a little.

Do write soon with your news.

Love, Jay

PAPUNYA
October 3rd, 1968

Dear Both of You,

Thursday night again and time for the weekly letter writing so I can take it to the Settlement office and drop it in the mailbag for the plane. It's such a rare thing for a plane here that whenever the Flying Doctor arrives for a patient, or whenever a visitor flies in the children all rush screaming to the classroom windows. They even know which plane is which.

Well, I've had almost a week with my own class. Although it's nice to feel 'in harness' once again I'm beginning to realise what an awfully hard time I've let myself in for. I think I used to complain about the discipline at Hawthorns [a school in Manchester, England] but it was heaven compared to the behaviour here. I'm convinced though that the fault lies in the whole set-up of these schools. Children who have only been out of the bush for two years are expected to sit at their desks all day long writing sums and working in a language that is completely foreign to them. I think that they should be doing practical work, where they can move about the room doing things which have some meaning for them. But there is simply no equipment. The way everyone else treats them and the way I shall maybe have to treat them too is to knock them around the ears. Well, that's only figuratively speaking but you know what I mean. Otherwise I will have a riot on my hands. If I didn't love the life up here so much I should be away on the next plane! But I will stick it for a little longer. Things can't get worse! I've been given the worst class too, boys and girls of 13 and 14 in their last year before going into Manual Training classes.

Sports went well last week. I got quite sunburnt from being out in the sun for two whole days. The weather is getting hotter now. My classroom was 90 degrees at 4 o'clock this afternoon.

Last weekend I got hold of a week old newspaper and saw that you had been having terrible floods in the south-east of England. Essex was actually mentioned by name so I do hope that everything is alright. At least the sea can't come in because you have those high cliffs and you are not near a river that might flood. Take care of yourselves. I think of you a lot.

Love, Jay

PAPUNYA
February 27th, 1969

Dear Both of You,

Well, we seem to have settled down to a season of overcast skies, occasional rain though heavy enough to block the roads for days at a time, and cooler temperatures. The cooler temperatures are quite a welcome change. I've dug up a patch at the side of the flat, about 12'x12', just to plant some vegetables. Peter gave me some wire to put around to keep out the camp dogs. When I dig in blood-and-bone fertilizer it attracts anything on four legs to roll in it. I could never have imagined anything growing in this brick red soil but I've seen such lovely lettuces and cabbages that I'm quite enthusiastic. I only hope the Aborigines don't pull them up.

We had two scares last week. You see, there are four flats in a block with an open courtyard in the middle. I'm in Flat 4 looking out to the bush and the mountain range. Very beautiful. But John in Flat 1 had a brown snake which had crawled under his front door while he was writing letters. Kelly and I bravely stood on a table and threw saucepan lids at it under the bed while John waited, hoe in hand, to decapitate it. Which he eventually did. But the head part wriggled half way down the length of the flat before dying and the tail wiggled until midnight, so he said! That was Thursday. On Saturday morning Liz, in Flat 2, came screaming across that there was a snake outside her back door. It was a death adder curled up fat and full after a meal. John raked it out, chopped it up, and it hardly wriggled. So now we all walk very warily at night. If we leave an outside light on moths and beetles are attracted. We've decided that snakes are the lesser of two evils and walk around in the dark.

Did I tell you I've adopted a cat of Shirley's? It's having kittens too I think. I really want a cattle dog and am awaiting one from a litter. The cat is light tabby and is very sweet. It just comes in for an evening meal and spends most of the time out. If it's raining I let it spend the night inside.

School is going down better this term. The little ones are easier to handle than the older ones though still very wild.

Love, Jay

When GENEVIEVE EDWARDS *(now Faulkner) wrote this rather alarming letter home from school camp, her parents read between the lines and realised it was more to do with undeclared homesickness than the horrors of school camp. Genevieve (pictured) was eleven at the time and a Year 7 student at Gippsland Grammar in Sale, Victoria. The camp was at Glenmaggie Weir in Central Gippsland. Genevieve clearly recovered her enthusiasm for travel, as she grew up to become a successful press photographer with the* Herald-Sun *in Melbourne. She now lives in Sydney with her husband, Brett Faulkner, a photographer with* The Australian *newspaper, and their two small sons. This letter was contributed by Genevieve's mother, Dianna Edwards, of Briagolong, Victoria.*

Dear Mum, Dad and Nicky,

How are you? I am alright I suppose. Apart from being tired and sore. I am in a 2-bed room with Carolyn.

Monday we went to Glenmaggie we walked over the wall. We later went swimming in a river the water was freezing we had a mud bath that was alright but we had to wash it off.

We have 3 courses for tea. On Monday we had soup for the first course. It looked like sick. I didn't have any. Tuesday night (tonight) we had soup again. It was different. I didn't have any.

We went on a 3 mile hike it was so awful my desert boots have got a hole in them. It's not too bad.

We have room 13 and nothing but bad luck has happened. I knocked the top off my toe on a bed.

Tonight we had a fancy hat party. Me, Carolyn, Debbie and Heather made one together. We stuck four towels together and made paper flowers out of tissues. We won our prize. We each got a Lifesaver.

This camp is so boring it seems like Friday already.

Love Gen

HELEN COOK *(now Cushing) was 22 when she arrived at the Gordon Base Camp in January 1983 to add her voice to the campaign against the damming of Tasmania's Franklin River wilderness area. Inspired by a speech by Bob Brown, and having recently completed her horticultural studies, she took a plane to Hobart and travelled 'up-river' to the blockade camp, where she became kitchen co-ordinator. The prime minister of the day, Malcolm Fraser, had refused to intervene in what had become Australia's biggest environmental battle. When Bob Hawke won office one of the first things he said in his historic acceptance speech was 'The Franklin dam will not be built.'*

Helen, who was eventually arrested at the blockade, is now Publishing and Merchandise Coordinator for Gardening Australia *at the ABC in Tasmania and is the author of the ABC* Book of Gardening for Kids. *She went on to marry Philip Cushing, who is mentioned by his nickname Philippe in the letter, and the couple now live with their two children in Hobart. Philip is a wilderness guide while Helen's kitchen co-worker, 'Rolly' (Roland Browne), is a lawyer in Hobart. This letter was contributed by Helen's father, Peter Cook, of Queenscliff, Sydney.*

1983
The Franklin Blockade as seen from the Kitchen
Sunday 16th January

Dear Folks,

It must be pretty late on a wet Sunday evening. I've just had an exhausted sort of a snooze – the kind that can't wait till bedtime but sort of merge into the same thing.

Did I tell you that Rolly and I are co-ordinating the kitchen? We must have fed 100 people tonight from our 'Shellite' stoves and burnt pots. Restaurant name – 'The Gordon Bleu: Wild Rivers Cuisine'. The patrons are impressed, the chefs are exhausted. It's not the cooking that's tiring – that's fun and creative – it's the constant demands people place on kitchen people. You sure find out about everyone when you're in a kitchen. It's a bit of a free for all at times and how can you refuse them, cold and wet and trying to save the wilderness?

There's been a build up of people over the last 3 days as there have been no actions and so very few arrests, but each day a boatload has arrived. This means we've gained more than we've lost, so the place is crawling. They're all saving up for tomorrow – the big day – get arrested with David Bellamy, let the world see you break the law, the laws of convenience which this crazy system has devised for its own irrational purposes. It's weird when you look at this whole scene in perspective. Standard question – 'Are you getting arrested tomorrow?' Answer: 'Yes.' Next: 'Are you going to gaol?' 'Are you coming back?' After a life time of being conditioned against arrest and gaol, it's a standard, respectable thing. I guess if you were in the army you'd be wondering who might get killed the next day. There's always some that don't come back.

And this arrest disease is infectious. I wouldn't feel complete if I left this blockade without being arrested. But I'm not into a big media event arrest. If I get arrested it'll be with a close friend strumming a guitar on Warner's Landing. I'll just tell Rolly so that he can cook dinner without me till I get back. Arrest for me would be a very personal, private matter – a simple comment to show the river and the forest that I care and to get those arrest statistics into 4 figures and round off my blockade experience – a day in the life of a kitchen co-ordinator at the Butler Island Base Camp, Lower Gordon River, The Middle of Nowhere.

I wake up, take the first part of the morning slowly, because it's my own private time. Have some muesli, write a letter, brush my teeth, put on the layers of wool and japara, think a while and head for the community area. Slosh through the mud, the sticks on the path sink within a day. We've had no sunshine since I got here. Rain is just part and parcel. This dampness is why the forest is what it is, so it doesn't really concern me. At least I don't have to worry about a sunburnt nose.

Wander up to the community area, discover it's later than I thought, avoid a tactics meeting or two or three or four, read some Thoreau, listening to Phillipe strum some tunes, prepare for the arrival of the 'J.

Lee M.', our boat. If there's action on, the scenario is different. Dash down to the barge to cheer as arrestees go by in a police boat, sing and chant as a bulldozer floats by like an idol, surrounded by police protection. Sometimes I get a jaunt in a boat or duckie. Not often enough. Perhaps a wander in the woods.

Then the 'J. Lee M.' arrives. From then on I change gear. New food arrives – it must be stored. Where? Make somewhere. New people. They don't know how things run so they ask heaps of moronic questions and expect hot water all the time. The patience I learnt from my mother and the detachment I learnt from the ashram come in handy. Stash the new food; begin organising people to chop for dinner. And all the time a constant barrage of questions, offers, unwanted suggestions, bread, can I have some bread, they all ask. Conversations are never completed. Names are always forgotten. Refill the Shellite tanks, put wood on the fire, eyes weeping from onions, dried out from the disinfectant in the hand wash water, haul a bucket of water up the pulley from the river; 'yes, you can chop this', 'grate this', 'peel this', 'chop it smaller', 'chop it bigger', 'chop it chop it chop it'.

'You know me from somewhere?' 'You're getting arrested tomorrow?' 'Ask Rolly.' 'Ask Rolly.' 'Ask Rolly.' 'Ask Helen.' 'Ask Helen.' 'Ask Helen.' We've got no time. Shellite's a dollar a litre. 'Fruit is outside.' 'You look cold and wet and weary – here's a treat for you.' Favouritism thrives. I know who deserves it and they get the best we can give. Too many cabbages and potatoes. Too much margarine – send us some milk powder. Send us honey, honey, honey. Boxes of licorice, homemade bread, we eat better than the Strahan camp. They send us all the munchies from their oven – bread and slices and all sorts. Got to keep up morale on the river. There ain't no corner store at the Gordon/Franklin junction.

The P.L.O. – Platypus Liberation Organisation. The Rainbow Warriors. A.S.I.O. The Greenkeepers. S.L.A.G., W.A.G., D.A.G., N.A.G., K.A.O.S. They come and go, interminably, affinity group after affinity group – N.V.A. trained and japara clad. From Strahan to Franklin, from Franklin to Queenstown to Risdon, and then back to Strahan. Cannon fodder. Most people see themselves as cannon fodder. Not me. I perform support functions. It's all 'functions', mind you, not roles. The dreaded roles are out, functions are in.

On with the day. Once it's all cooking I just have to check the pots and tell people there's nothing to do. Then around 6pm, clang the gong, collect the money, serve it up, skip dinner myself and disappear. EXIT. The clean up is their concern. I just burn the pots.

Adios amigos. I think of you between cloves of garlic.

Much love,
Helen

AFTERWORD

In these days of speedy email communication, the handwritten letter is a rarity, even though postal volumes have continued to grow over recent years. Yet letters are unique forms of expression that go beyond recording events over time and generations.

If you think about it, handwritten letters are as distinctive as their authors' fingerprints; by putting pen to paper we relate in ways that are far more personal and ultimately more revealing than any other form of communication.

Just imagine the sheer emotion during the war years when letters arrived at distant battlefields. Receiving news from home was important, but it was the sight of that familiar handwriting – the neatly formed characters or the wayward scrawl – and the fact the letter had been smoothed and folded by a friend or loved one, that 'spoke' on a deeper level. And letters are saved, whereas emails tend to disappear.

The heartfelt letters in this wonderful and moving collection have brought joy and comfort to many Australians over vast distances.

Australia Post is proud to be connecting people in this memorable and lasting way. To provide a service that touches people's hearts is always a privilege.

Graeme John
Managing Director, Australia Post

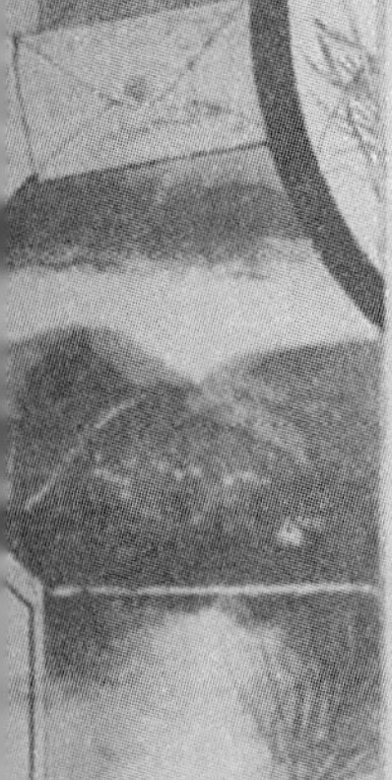

OLD CHRISTMAS?

OLD Christmas? No,—
Though States and Kingdoms wear,
And change and ruin grow
From ages as they flew;
He's as light of tread, as young and fair,
As a thousand years ago.
The morning beams are always new,
And scatter blessings free;
And the Christmas Day
Is as new as they.
He shall never part with his youth of heart,
While there's love in this world below.

MACKAY.

INDEX